D0044447

Precious Thoughts from the Heart

Precious Thoughts from the Heart

THE PRAYER-POEMS OF

Ruth Harms Calkin

INSPIRATIONAL PRESS

New York

First Inspirational Press edition published in 1994.

Inspirational Press
A division of BBS Publishing Corporation
386 Park Avenue South
New York, NY 10016

Inspirational Press is a registered trademark of BBS Publishing Corporation.

Published by arrangement with Tyndale House Publishers, Inc.

Library of Congress Catalog Card Number: 94-77199
ISBN: 0-88486-101-5

Text and jacket designed by Cindy LaBreacht.
Printed in the United States of America.

Contents

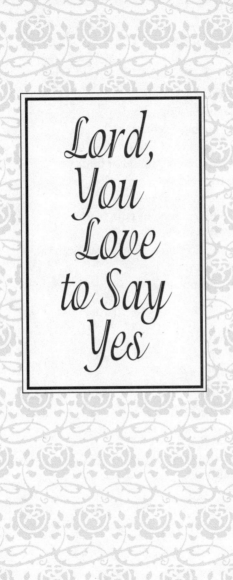

Lord,
You
Love
to Say
Yes

I Love It, Lord

What in the world
Is going on today, Lord?
Why the big celebration?
The fragrance of lilacs
The shimmering sound of birds
The red-gold sky
The air blue and sweet
The sudden burst of pink bloom
A thirsty vine
The shout of mountains miles around...
Really, Lord
What's happening?

Is it—
Could it be
That Spring has made her debut?
Is that why
You've dressed all of Nature
In party clothes?

Whatever the reason
I love it, Lord.
Thank You!

Plain Old Me

O Lord
Here I am again
Just plain old me
Coming to You
As I've come a thousand times—
And this is what always happens:
Your response is immediate
You open Your arms unhesitatingly
You draw me to Yourself
You clasp me to Your Father-heart.
Then You reaffirm my position:
I'm a child of the King
And all that is Yours is mine.
When I begin my stammering account
Of gross unworthiness
Your gentle smile hushes me.
With endless patience
You remind me once more
That my value never determines Your love.
Rather, Your love determines my value.

Illusive Dreams

Sometimes, Lord
I think I spend my entire life
Working toward illusive dreams.
I dream that someday things will be
Exactly as I want them:
I'll ride on the crest
Of my noble achievements.
With an easygoing independence.
I'll keep my confident cool
My house will stay spotless
My budget will balance
My family will applaud me
My friends will acclaim me
I'll grow with charisma.
Lord, am I missing the mark?
Is there a chance for my dreams?

Child of My Plan
Seek first the Kingdom of God
And His righteousness
And every plan of Mine
Will exceed by far
All your illusive dreams.

How Else?

O Lord
I am continually amazed
At Your willingness to work
Through my nothingness
And my simplicity.
I am always suggesting
That You wait
Until some future spring or fall
When I can offer You
A more polished, glittering self—
But the very things I struggle
To correct and improve
You want surrendered as they are.
You want to give Yourself
A magnificent reputation
By Your accomplishment in me.
So, dear Lord
Take my insignificance
And make it a shining emblem
Of Your creative power.
Do it all by Yourself.

Dear child, how else
Would it ever get done?

The Facade

Lord, I bow before You contritely
Confessing my shameful failures.
This whole wretched week
I've felt like a phony
And my actions have justified
My gnawing guilt.

Monday:
I spoke at a women's luncheon
And repeatedly emphasized
The joy of gentleness,
Then two hours later
I was angrily shouting at Jennifer.

Tuesday:
My widowed neighbor invited me in
For a cup of coffee.
I was simply "too busy."
Later that day I learned
Her beloved niece had been killed.

Wednesday:
"I'll pray as you have your checkup,"
I told my concerned friend.

Thursday:
My friend stopped by to thank me
For the prayer I neglected to pray.

Friday:
Over the phone I said sweetly:
"Don't give it a thought.
It's perfectly all right."
I was thinking—*how stupidly careless.*

Saturday:
I was tight with tension
Bone tired.
I was sure Aunt Sarah would call
So I didn't answer the phone.

Sunday:
Reverently sitting
In this quiet sanctuary
I wince to think of my subtle facade.
Purge me, Lord.
Shatter my pretense
Make me a glowing demonstration
Of the hymns I sing today
With such holy joy.

Lord, You Love To Say Yes

Lord, I asked You for abundant life
Rich, challenging, full of adventure
And You said Yes.
I asked You for an undisturbable joy
Independent of transitory change
And You said Yes.
I asked You to thread my tears into a song
When I was shattered and torn with grief
And You said Yes.
I asked You to steady me when I staggered—
To hold me when I struggled
To seize me when I resisted
And You said Yes.
I asked You to forgive my vain grasping
My foolish fears, my willful pride
And You said Yes.
I asked You to be my Helper, my Friend
My light in the darkness
And You said Yes.
I asked You to guide me all my life
With Your wisdom, Your counsel
Your captivating love
And You said Yes.
Sometimes, Lord
I feel like a spoiled child
Who gets whatever he asks for.
You overwhelm me with joy
For *You love to say Yes!*

Think of Me

For so many days
I've struggled with this hurt
The cutting words
The stinging resentment.
I *thought* she was my friend
I trusted her, upheld her
And now there is this stone wall
Of suspicion and distrust.
Oh, Lord
Such betrayal of friendship
Baffles and overwhelms me.
I'm haunted by the memory
Of her angry eyes
Her flaming face.
She left me gasping for breath—
So unfair was her accusation.
Yet—even now, dear Lord
The words I read so long ago
Come ringing like a distant bell:
"Let it be—think of Me."
Lord, empower me to do *this* day
What I know I must do ultimately
If Your love is my highest goal.

Let it be—think of Me.

Sorry, Lord

Lord
That woman I had lunch with
Seems to be an authority
On every conceivable subject.
She quotes statistics
Faster than a secretary
Clicks typewriter keys.
There's no in-between for her:
She's vehemently for
Or vehemently against.
She knows where to shop
How to shop, when to shop.
She knows who's in and what's out.
Her vocabulary is stupendous.
(I wonder if she can spell the words?)
If you like ruffles and frills
She's beautifully groomed.
Her jewelry is authentic—
Anything but costume jewelry.
Just the same, Lord
I doubt that she can bake
An apple strudel like mine.

Dear child
Is there something
You'd like to confess?

Phone Call

I answered the phone
And wished I hadn't.
Lord, she keeps talking and talking
And there's no way to stop her.
She asks a question
And gives her own answer.
In the middle of one story
She starts another.
Today she said lustily:
"Life is just rush rush rush."
I prayed that she'd rush
To her kitchen.

Lord, when she calls I feel trapped—
Pushed into a corner.
I want to say, "No, no
I haven't the time today."
Yet when I think of Your patience
I am gnawed by guilt.
Is it a false guilt, Lord?
I honestly think my emotions
Are more harmed
Than hers are helped.
Am I wrong?

Tell me, please tell me...
How would *You* handle such calls?

Celebration

When I think of Your lavish goodness
The longings You've satisfied
The forgiveness You've granted
The promises You've kept
When I think of Your irresistible love
Your ceaseless care
Your unfailing protection...

O Lord God
I want to raise flags
And fly banners
And sound bugles.
I want to run with lighted torches
And praise You
From the mountaintop.
I want to write symphonies
And shout for joy.
I want to throw a festive party
For ten thousand guests.
I want to celebrate with streamers
And bright lights
And an elaborate banquet.

Fine, dear child.
I'm ready.

You Are Free

O God
I read today
That the sons of Jacob
And their descendants
Had lived in Egypt 430 years.
But on the last day
Of the 430th year
Your people left Egypt
And the cruel bondage
They had painfully endured.
This was the time You selected.
God, what time have You selected
To free me from the cruel tyranny
That binds me without mercy to myself?

Chosen child
In My Son
You are even now
Completely free.
Accept your freedom!
Walk out this very moment
Into the radiant company
Of My people.

The Time Is Now

Lord
I see with startling clarity
That life is never long enough
To put You off
Until tomorrow.
The things that are before
Are all too soon behind.
I can never pick up
The years I've put down.
If I intend
To walk with You tomorrow
I must start today.

Earthbound

Tonight
My heart is hushed with quiet
Through and through
A gentle stillness permeates our house.
I rest contentedly by my husband's side
As though I hadn't a care in the world.

Except...

I *know* I'll hear
That loud earth-jarring truck
At six o'clock in the morning
When the men pick up trash
On our street.

Lord, I'm so earth-bound.

Final Decision

In this agonizing crisis, Lord
When my husband is jolted
By the twisted turn of events
And everything seems to be wrong
I desperately long to help him.
I ache to break the intense pressure—
To lessen the hurt and confusion.
Yet all I can do is listen.
I can be a sounding board
While he bounces back
Frustrations, fears, feelings.
I can be at his side
When he comes home depleted.
I can *pray* what I can't possibly *say*
For deep within me
I know the final decision
Has to be his.

Lord, that's not true:
The final decision
Has to be Yours.

Birthday Dinner

Here we are—just the two of us
Sitting across the table from each other
In this quaint old restaurant
With its nostalgic charm.
O Lord
When my husband called to say
He had planned a birthday celebration
I had no idea we'd be coming here.
How pleasant it is, how peaceful
To relax without feeling pressured
To chatter aimlessly, happily
To laugh at our own foolish jokes...

As we wait for our entree
In the flickering candleglow
My thoughts are ribboned with tenderness.
How is it possible, dear Lord
How is it possible
That we should still feel
This dear mysterious newness
After so many years of marriage?
But that's the way it is with You:
The best is always just beginning.

Never Alone

Lord God...
As I sit here silently
With my friend of many years
Please let her know how deeply I care.
How achingly I long to comfort
Her grief-stupored heart.
Make me just now a gentle transmitter
Of Your calming peace.
Her anguish is too deep for words—
At least my words, Lord.
She needs the solace of *Your* words
Whispered assuringly to her waiting heart.
In her new-born pain
You alone can sustain her.
In the long, tedious climb from rock bottom
You alone can stabilize her.

Without You there is only despair
But praise upon praise
She is never without You!

I Listen...

God, without You
I am like a blind man
Groping to find my way
In the darkness.
Voices are calling from this place
And voices are calling from that place
But I am confused—
I don't know where to turn.

Always I listen for Your voice
For You alone bring light
To my desolate being.

Still I brood and grope
In the darkness
As voices calling from this place
And voices calling from that place
Make the absence of Your voice
Ever more painful.

"And I will give thee the treasures of darkness...."

(Isaiah 45:3)

All Will Be Well

O Lord God
In the midst of consuming sorrow
When despair and loneliness hedge me in
You understand my frailties—
My hesitancies, my fears.
As I scamper from doubt to doubt
You forgive so quickly my outbursts.
Never do You drive me away
When I rail against You
In peevish rebellion.
When I scream
"Don't you even care?"
You quiet my fragmented heart.
You work in me silently
Always planning in love.
You refine me in the white-flamed
Furnace of affliction.
In the silent darkness You whisper:
Trust Me—all will be well.

He Said—She Said

Another marriage is shattered, Lord.
The divorce will be final next week.

He said it was the breakdown of communication
And the subtle infiltration of boredom.
She said it was an accumulation of things.
He said she was unnecessarily preoccupied
With home and children and activities.
She said he stifled her dreams
And ignored her achievements.
He said he felt imprisoned, restricted—
That night after night he got the old push-away.
She said he was harsh and brutal
And he often embarrassed her in public.
He said her critical attitudes
Contributed to his sense of inadequacy.
She said she felt lonely and unappreciated
With no claim to personal identity.
He said she wallowed in self-pity
And refused to acknowledge her benefits.
She said he was thriftless and irresponsible.
He said she didn't understand.
She said he didn't care.

Lord, how tragic.
Through all the wearisome years
Neither of them asked what *You* said.

Sacred Assignment

Lord
Here in my narrow hospital bed
I wait with brooding apprehension.
I trusted You exclusively
I prayed with fervent supplication.
I had so achingly hoped
You would touch and heal me
Without medication
Without the aid of man.
Wouldn't this give You great glory?
Wouldn't this enhance Your reputation?
I'm perplexed, Lord
I'm entangled in brambles of doubt
Surely You can extricate me...

Dear child, listen!
I have a plan for your doctor, too.
I have given him the sacred assignment
Of becoming My instrument of healing
As we work together in your behalf.
So trust Me to create a double joy:
Yours and his.

Help Them Just Now

I keep thinking of them, Lord
Thinking and thinking...

Sitting in the booth next to theirs
I heard but fragments
Of their troubled conversation.
She reproached him
For his thoughtlessness
His shameful unconcern.
With hatred in his voice
He whirled his bitter accusations—
Then he grabbed the check
And left her sitting there alone.
I wonder—is she still alone
This cold and rainy night?

Forgive me, Lord
Please forgive me...

Too often I take for granted
The days
The nights
The gentle moments in-between
When my husband holds me close
And softly whispers:
"God was good to give me you."

Subtle Reminder

O Lord, thank You!
I love the way You teach me.

Remember how it happened?
I was quietly reading from Timothy:
"But godliness with contentment
Is great gain."
Then in the middle of lamenting
My own personal battle
With discontent
Jimmy came bursting in.
Churning with excitement
He insisted on showing me
The newest addition
To his menagerie of bugs:
"A beetle that's a boy!"

I managed sufficient enthusiasm
To welcome the new family friend
Before going back to Timothy.
Then I read it again—
The verse on contentment.
Suddenly, Lord, I chuckled aloud
At Your subtle reminder:

Often it's easier to find
"A beetle that's a boy"
Than a Christian who's content.

Longer Than Tomorrow

"Look, Mom
I have to learn
This long list
By heart.
I've got to know it
By tomorrow
Will you help me?"

Lord
I too have a long list
To learn *by heart*.
Patience...
Contentment...
Trust...
On and on it goes.
Will You help me?

But, Lord
I'll need longer
Than tomorrow.

Paid in Full

It seemed so strange
To call a taxi today—
The first time in years!
With routine boredom
The driver set the meter
And the minutes began clicking away.
I watched closely
Hoping we'd avoid the detours
And at least some of the red lights.
Somehow, that meter clicked
With such persistent rapidity.
When I finally reached my destination
And paid the fare
I was thankful all over again
That I'm seldom without a car.
Thankful too, dear God
That when I reach
My heavenly destination
Your welcome words will be:
Paid in full!

My Radiant Dawn

Dear God
The psalmist David said
He watched for You
As one who waits for the dawn.

I know, God
I know...

One who waits for the dawn
Waits in quivering darkness
In loneliness
In somber silence...
He waits for that
Which comes slowly—
Ever so slowly...
But, God
He waits for that
Which he *knows* will come
And when it comes
At last there is light!

I am waiting
As David waited.
O God
You *will* come—
My Radiant Dawn!

While She Waits

Lord
They hadn't wanted it like this—
Nor had they anticipated
The sudden drastic change.
Faithfully, with infinite patience
He'd taken care of her
Day by day, year after year.
He'd fixed her meals
Helped her into her clothes—
Even combed her thinning hair.
He'd read to her by the hour
Written short notes
And fluffed the pillows
Behind her aching back.
Theirs was a beautiful devotion
And now he's gone
And she is so desperately lonely.
Today between choking sobs
She told me how she longed to join him.
Surely You understand, dear Lord.
Take her with You soon, I pray.
Give her her heart's desire.
And while she waits
May those of us who love her
Do what we can to make the lonely hours
A little less painful.

"Have a Nice Forever"

Even at longest, Lord
Life is fleetingly short—
A mere breath
A withering flower
A shadow in pantomime.
It sobers me
That I am but a passing occupant
A temporary guest who says hello
Then so suddenly—good-bye.

But, Lord
You have chosen me
To be Your very own.
The instant You call my name
I shall be a permanent resident
In my Father's house.
Once again
With ecstatic joy
I shall say hello—
But never through all Eternity
Shall I have to say good-bye!

The Trust of the Unexplained

Lord of my aching heart:
He was so young
So very young
With all of life before him.
Exuberant, vital
Full of promise, of breathless wonder.
Gifted, intelligent, sensitive
Always inquisitive
Eager to learn, to know, to do.
A dreamer, a schemer
Eyes full of merriment
Heart full of laughter
Venture in his blood
Mischief in his fingers
Challenge in his thoughts
So many plans, so many hopes
Admired by his teachers
Extolled by his friends
Loved, so dearly loved...

Lord, no longer dare I beat my fists
Upon the walls of Heaven.
I am too weary, too sorrow-consumed.
I know now that ten thousand whys
Will never bring him back.
In pitch darkness I have shouted my whys.
My reward? A sea of shadowed silence.
What is left?
What more shall I ask?
Just this dear God:
Think through me Your thoughts
Create within me Your peace
Until there is born in my aching heart
"The trust of the unexplained."

Majestic Approval

O God
I'd love to keep
The beauty of this day
Forever and forever:
The sky incredibly blue
New leaves shining
Flowers swaying
In the gentle breeze
Birds with changeful wills
Darting here and there
The lake a sparkling jewel
Surrounded by spicy pines
And You looking down
At Your handiwork
With majestic approval.

Happy New Year

This very first day
Of the fresh new year
I sing a new song—
A joyful, exalted song!
With Israel's sweet singer I exclaim:
"How good it is to sing God's praise
How delightful and how right."
The volume increases
The tempo accelerates.
With glorious anticipation
I shout a rousing welcome
To the up-and-coming days.
The future cannot daunt me
Every inscrutable mystery
Becomes a consolation of joy
For with You in control, dear God
The worst may happen
But the best is yet to come.

New Recipe

Thank You, Lord
For this luscious new salad
I'm preparing for our dinner—
And for the kindness of the friend
Who shared the recipe.
Thank You for the joy of creativity
For the satisfaction of achievement.
Thank You for sufficient money
To buy the necessary ingredients
For the blue bowl I'm using
To mix and season
For the utensils to measure and stir.
Thank You for the eagerness to sample it
For the hunger to relish it
For the health to digest it.
Thank You for the anticipation of my family
And for the excitement over a new recipe.
Thank You for their expressive appreciation:
"Wow, Mom! This is terrific."

Goodness, Lord
What a wealth of blessing
You've wrapped up
In one new salad.
Thank You!
Tonight at the dinner table
We'll remember to thank You again.

Enough Family

Really, Lord
He's a ridiculously
Homely little dog.
Look at him
With his drooping tail
And his crumpled ear.
Besides, if there's anything
We don't need around here
It's another dog.
But what could I do
Against an argument like this:
"Mother! How could you turn your back
On God's poor homeless creature?"
So, who's pouring warm milk
For God's poor homeless creature?
Me—the mother who vehemently declared:
"No more dogs!"
Lord, if he belongs to somebody
Please help us to find out soon.

After all—
One husband three children
Two dogs two cats
One parakeet four goldfish
And a pet lizard
That frightens me to death—
Isn't that enough family
For one mother to manage?

Lord,
I Keep
Running
Back
To You

I Keep Running Back To You

You know how it is with me, Lord:
So often I mess up my days.
I judge harshly
I am critical and obstinate
I waste time and energy
I blame others for my failure.
There are people I try to avoid
And tasks I try to evade
And when I can't have my own way
I sulk in my own little corner.
Lord, I even turn my back on You
To escape Your penetrating gaze.

Then finally I get fed up with myself.
The intolerable loneliness frightens me
And I can no longer endure my shame.
It always happens, Lord—
I keep running back to You!

Where else can I go?
Who else understands me so well
Or forgives me so totally?
Who else can save me from foolish pride?
No one, Lord, but You.
So thank You for accepting me
For loving me
For always welcoming me.
I just can't help it, Lord.
I keep running back to you!

The Facts

Lord
When I feel I can't possibly make it
When I feel deluged with problems
When I feel helpless
Against the strange twistings of life
When I feel there is no way out
The FACT is
You have a Plan
You know what You're about.
The FACT is
The greater the strategy of the Enemy
The greater the assurance of victory.
The FACT is
The worst may seem to happen
But the best is on the way.
God, hold me to the facts.

Rivers and Rivers

O my Father
My heart longs for You!
Fill me to capacity with Your Spirit...
No, Father, I'm sorry—
That's not sufficient.
Fill me to *overflowing* with Your Spirit
And then increase my capacity
That there might be still more overflow.
Out of my life
May there flow rivers
And rivers
And still more rivers
Of Living Water
Bringing relief, release
And exhilarating refreshment
To a bruised and broken world
Where thirst can never be quenched
Apart from You.

Rare Moments
of Delight

Because You are God
And Your Word is unquestionable
There are things I assuredly know
Even when my heart is a brambled desert
And every ounce of emotion is drained:
I know Your love is everlasting
I know You will never forsake me
Nor will You leave me comfortless
I know I may come to You boldly
I know You will teach and instruct me
You will guide me with Your eye
I know my past is forgiven
And my future is secure.
But oh, dear God
How I praise You for the marvel
Of those rare, mysterious moments
When suddenly, without a flash or a sound
You add to my *knowing*
The ecstasy of *feeling*
And I am lifted to peaks of delight!

Unexpected Reply

Lord, dear Lord
I'm desperately pleading with you.
Please, please speak to my husband.
You see, he's made a determined decision
And I'm convinced he's totally wrong.
Change his mind, Lord.
Nudge him, prick him
Turn him around, anything—
But capture his attention
And show him I'm right.

Foolish child, don't ask Me
To make your husband
What you want him to be.
Just ask Me to make him
What I want him to be.

Oh, Lord...
Then You must work on me.

The Answer

Lord
Sometimes Your answers come
With startling swiftness
Or sometimes the waiting is long...

Our friends with a fast-growing family
Consulted a realtor on Tuesday
And on Wednesday their house was sold.
Their hearts are full of praise to You.

Our friends four blocks from us
Are equally anxious to sell.
Their need for a larger house is urgent.
Six different times, dear Lord
Their dreams faded
As negotiations fell through.
Yet they are firmly convinced
That Your love encompasses
Every test and disappointment.
Their hearts are full of praise to You.

Thank You for both families
And for their authentic witness
To the power of praise—
When You say Yes
When You say No
When You say Wait.

I Know Who I Am

There he sat on his front porch
(Probably three or four years old)
And when he flashed a merry smile
I stopped to ask his name.
"I'm my daddy's boy," he said, grinning
And then he was off to play,
I still don't know his name, Lord
But it doesn't matter.
He knows who he is
And that makes everything all right.

Thank You, Lord
With all my heart
That I may say with genuine confidence
"I'm my Father's child."
That makes everything all right.

Seek First

O Lord
How futile, how foolish
To attempt to keep up with the Joneses
On the gold-studded ladder of success.
Even if we make it
(Setting high, competitive goals)
We awake one dismal morning
To discover the Smiths have bypassed the Joneses
So it starts again—the goading competition.

God, Your objective is far more rewarding.
You want us to "keep up" with Your Plan
For our individual lives.
"Seek first the Kingdom of God"
Is Your shining word to us.
Forgive us for moments and days
(Even months)
When our love of money
Has exceeded our love for You.
Please, God
Be our Financial Advisor
And deliver us from a thousand "if onlys."
May we never be defeated
By the lack of money
Or captivated by the lure of it.

Marriage Formula

I read all these books on marriage
And sometimes I feel like a colossal failure.
I just don't always make it to the door
With a rosebud in my hair
When my husband comes home from work.
(After all, we have only one rosebush.)
I don't always remember to salt the eggs
Or pick up the suit from the cleaners
And often, too often
My mascara looks streaked.
But Lord, do You know what I pray for
Above all else in our marriage?
Just a walloping big heart of love—
A love that listens and understands
A love that accepts and forgives
A love that responds and trusts
And never once considers giving up.
Maybe that will make up for the rosebuds.

Exclusively Ours

Through all the years of marriage
We've happily shared with others:
Our home, food, laughter, tears.
We've shared friendships and confidences
We've shared appreciation
We've shared music, books, flowers
We've shared victories and defeats.
But God, You've given us one priceless gift
That belongs exclusively to us
Not to be shared with another—
The beautiful gift of physical intimacy.
Thank You for its mystery
Its wonder, its delight.
May we never mishandle it.
May we respect and cherish it always.
May our self-giving continue to be
An expression of oneness
A celebration of wholeness.
Keep it alive, fulfilling
And always full of surprises.
O God, what a marvelous expression
Of Your own fathomless love!

This Time

Hesitantly she asked
"Will you pray for me?"
Lord, her troubled, tear-filled eyes
Have haunted me ever since.
Oh, she is so young, so beautiful
And on her college campus
The walls against conviction stand so erect.
She is tortured by the knowledge
Of the reality of her guilt
But her struggle with temptation
Seems intolerable at times.
It comes, she said, in rhythmic waves.
It dazes, it taunts, it baffles her.

Speak to her tormented heart, Lord.
Comfort her, sustain and strengthen her.
Assure her of Your enabling power
To steady her against future assaults.
Help her to cling tenaciously
To an inescapable fact:
"No degree of temptation
Justifies any degree of sin."
You Yourself have promised
An immediate way of escape—
All the time
Every time
This time.

My Life Is Richer

How can I thank her, dear Lord
For what she did for me today?
How can I express my sudden release
Because she genuinely cared?
It was such a simple gesture, really—
A friendship card with a single line:
"My life is richer because of you."

You know, Lord, how numb I felt
Before the mail arrived.
Morning came much too soon
And I awakened weary, depleted.
For some unaccountable reason
Our house looked dismal and drab.
Most of the morning I berated myself
And fought a losing battle with doubt.
Then I heard the mailman.

O God, is it really true?
Is someone's life richer because of me?
Despite my whimpering
My defeats, my petty concerns
Am I usable in Your Kingdom, after all?
Suddenly, God, I believe that I am!

Forgive me for wasting a glorious morning
That should have been wrapped in praise.
Thank You especially for the friend
Who gathered my scattered emotions
And fused them into serenity
Without the slightest awareness of her mission.
Bless her abundantly, Lord
And please let her know
That *my* life is richer because of *her.*

It Takes Work

....

Brown eyes
Shiny hair
Blue jeans and sweater
Ten years old...

It was an excellent piano lesson
And I happily told her so.
Then I teasingly asked
"How did it happen?"
Her response was half smiling
Half indignant:
"It didn't just happen—I worked!"
What beautiful reassurance, Lord
Especially today—
Our wedding anniversary.
A positive vital marriage
Never just happens.
It takes renewed motivation
It takes commitment
It takes determination
It takes stupendous effort
It takes work!

Continual Discovery

Dear Lord
It sings in me again and yet again—
The ever-expanding joy, the fulfillment
Of living with my gentle husband.
For thirty-three years
He's thrown stardust in my eyes
And flowers in my path.
Just this morning I found a love note
Taped to the mirror in our bathroom
And one day last week he called to say
"In case you've forgotten, I love you!"

Through stumbling and victories
Through laughter and tears
We continue to discover
We're so right for each other.
Only You, dear Lord
Could have given so great a gift.

The Challenge

It may be true, dear God
That my husband and I had more to live on
A year ago than we have today
But it is equally true
That we have just as much to live *for*.
The real values of our lives remain
Solid, stable, unshifting.
Our financial loss has in no way
Diminished the value of a single friendship.
We have lost nothing of human dignity
And we are discovering spiritual realities
Full of wonder and sheer delight.
Our faith in Your loving-kindness
Adds growing serenity to our guided lives.
You are making us increasingly aware
That what we *are* is vastly more vital
Than our fondest possessions.
Above all, You are teaching us
That a limited salary is our shining challenge
To trust and exalt our limitless God!

Forgive Me

Lord
So often I am
Fearful
Unbelieving
And apologetic about my faith.
I analyze
Whittle down
And tear apart
Your very words.
I conjure foolish reasons
For my lack of trust
As though You couldn't possibly mean
What You so clearly said.
Yet, all the while You wait for me
To believe *exactly* what You said—
Without exception
Without alteration.
Forgive me for treating You
Like someone who would lie.

I Trust You

O God, I trust You.
I don't understand
I cannot begin to comprehend
The wisdom of Your way
In my torn and tangled life
But I am steadfastly believing
That Your plan for me today
Must be—
Surely it *must* be
As kind
As loving
As profitable
As Your plan for me
In joyful days now past.
You are the same
Yesterday
And today
And forever
So, dear God
I trust You.

The Only Thing

Thank You, thank You, God
For creating within me
An intense and powerful longing
For You...
You...
You...
Success doesn't matter anymore, Lord.
Rich or poor
Recognized or nameless
Win or lose
The only thing that matters
The *only* thing, dear Lord
Is to walk hand-in-hand
And heart-to-heart with You.
Nothing in my life
Has any real or lasting significance
Unless it relates to You.

You Did All the Rest

O Lord God!
I did what You asked me to do:
I just opened windows
Wide...
Wide...
And You did all the rest
You poured into my heart
A blessed, blissful contentment.
You saturate my mind
With gigantic thoughts of You.
You struck an artesan well within me
Until sheer joy sprang forth.
You led me out of the valley of despair
Into a succession of incredible happenings.
Problems which seemed insurmountable
Melted like wax before my eyes.
Fears faded away like threatening clouds.
You startled me
You amazed me
With the glory of Your revelation.
It is true
Gloriously true—
I have literally walked and breathed with God.
I just opened windows
Wide...
Wide...
God, You did all the rest!

I Felt Led

Forgive Me, Lord, for so often
Hiding under the protective covering
Of the words, "I felt led."
How convenient the phrase becomes—
How comforting
How soothing.
I've resorted to "I felt led"
When errors in judgment have betrayed me
When pride has swallowed me whole.
Under the subtle guise of "I felt led"
I've spent money recklessly
I've lashed out unmercifully
I've neatly evaded responsibility.

But today, Lord, I'm disturbed.
I've heard Your convicting voice
Persuading me that I dare not
Ride slipshod over others
In determining Your will.
I must seek Your guidance honestly
Without taking shortcuts
Or zooming in with push-button answers
Or kneeling on a cushion of "I felt led."
Teach me God-reliance, not self-reliance.
Above all, in seeking guidance
May I focus all my attention
On You, my Guide.

What's Myself Doing to Myself

With childish intensity she asked
"What's myself doing to myself?"
I couldn't help but smile
As she stood before the mirror
Struggling so impatiently
With a stubborn jacket zipper.

But I'm not smiling now, Lord
As I pass my own mirror
And glance at the tension
Etching my somber face.
I'm frightened, Lord.
Her innocent question clutches me:
"What's myself doing to myself?"

Frustrated, frantic
So often breathless
Too many irons in the fire...
What am I doing to my body—
To my mind, my emotions?
What am I doing to my family?

What am I doing to Your Plan
For my personal fulfillment?
Why do I live like this, Lord
As though Your world
Couldn't exist without me?
Why do I so often
Tear myself from Your control?

Dear Lord, calm me.
Pull me off the merry-go-round
Of converging conflicts.
Give balance to my boggled mind.
This very hour, Lord
Infuse me with Your poise and power
Until my total self
Is submerged in You—Yourself.
Only then will I be free
To be myself.

Usable

Lord, this is one of those "blob-days"
When I feel useless and ineffective.
Somehow, I feel totally unrelated
To a world of people who need You.
I hear preachers, talented musicians
And women who speak at luncheon clubs
Whose Christian witness excites and challenges.
Hundreds of lives are changed, renewed
Because of their dynamic message.

I too want to live for You radiantly.
I want to be Your instrument
In motivating and revitalizing others.
But nothing I do seems to reach very far.
To tell the truth, I feel quite unnecessary.
Did I miss Your instructions
Or is there nothing for me to do?

Fretting child
I did not call you to flaunt your talents
I called you to serve Me sincerely
Where, when, and how I choose.
If you are usable, you will be used.
It is to your great spiritual advantage
That you don't know to what extent.

Oh, How We Praise You, God

Oh, how we praise You, God
For the marvel of our differences.
I am a woman—
First and foremost a woman.
I have a woman's understanding
A woman's discernment and empathy
A woman's emotional response.
My husband is a man—
First and foremost a man.
He has a man's practicality
A man's logic and perception
A man's ambition.
Equal in value and dignity?
Assuredly!
Nevertheless, we function differently.
We express differently.
We react differently.
"Male and female created He them."
This fact we cannot change
Nor do we want to.
Oh, how we praise You, God
For the marvel of our differences
And for the wisdom of Your plan.

His Part—My Part

Lord
You want me to trust you so totally
That I am unmoved by any circumstance:
Then work in me that steadfast trust.
You want me to choose to do right:
Then turn me from wanting any plan but Yours.
You want me to revere and honor You:
Then refresh and revive me.
You want me to obey You uninterruptedly:
Then make Your Word my guide.
You want me to depend upon You increasingly:
Then reassure me that Your promises are mine.
You want Your will to be my will:
Then help me to love Your every wish.

I expect Your help, dear Lord
For You've never broken a single promise
And You're not going to start with me.

Consolation

He is old.
His hair is silver-white.
Day after day
for eight dreary months
He walked from his home
To the hospital six blocks away.
Day after day
He sat by her bedside
Gently stroking her feeble hand.
Only occasionally did she recognize him
Or know he was there.
But when she responded
With just a trace of a smile
Tears of elation filled his shadowed eyes.

A week ago Tuesday
He walked to the hospital
For the last time.
Had she lived but one more week
They would have observed
Their sixtieth wedding anniversary.

Until You take him, Lord
May his own consoling words
Be his great sustaining force:
*"We've had longer together
Than we'll ever have apart."*

Prodigal Daughter

Again, dear Lord
I pray for the dear distraught mother
Who called me early this morning.
Thoughts of her keep hovering
And I feel thrust into the midst
Of her fear and bewilderment.

In a tense and turbulent scene
Her daughter shouted with savage anger:
"I don't care what you say—
I'll never come home, never!"
And now the mother is torn and tortured
With the bitter memory
Of clashing wills and crushing words.
She maligns herself relentlessly, Lord.
She wonders if she asked too much
Or denied too much
Or gave too much.
Perhaps she was too lenient
Or at times too harsh
Or too often absorbed in her own interests.
Over and over she rehashes it.

O God
With all her gnawing guilt
Help her to see
That none of her blundering questions
Will bring her daughter home.
She needs to turn her thoughts
From her blunders to Your blessings—
From her despair to Your deliverance.
Though her dreams lie lifeless
Enable her even now to trust You.
Touch her songless heart with hope
And remind her often, Lord
That when You spoke of the Prodigal Son
you meant a daughter, too.

Which Part of Him Went to Heaven?

Lord...dear Lord
Which part of him went to heaven?
My heart cries out to know.
Was it his laughing eyes?
His sandy hair?
His boyish grin?
But, Lord—
I saw them put that part of him
Far, far beneath the black earth.

Was it his awareness, Lord?
That part of him
That chose blue ties
And rare steaks
and symphonies?
Even that part that
Worried
Struggled
Dreamed?
Perhaps—
But his blue ties look drab
As they hang without life
And symphonies sound like funeral songs.

O dear Lord
I so long to know:
Which part of him went to heaven?

Was it his intense conviction?
His secret longings?
The challenges he so nobly accepted?

Was it his ever-deepening belief
That life has significance—
That You are total Reality?

Please tell me, Lord—
Which part of him went to heaven?

"I will...receive you unto myself; that where I am,
there ye may be also" (John 14:3).

God's Searchlight

O God
If suddenly You were to reveal
To my family, my friends, my neighbors
Every real thought behind my courteous words
If You were to point to my clenched fist
While my other hand is openly extended
If You were to bring to light
Every masked motive, every selfish act
I would cringe with remorse
And beg You to remove Your light of revelation.
Yet, Lord, when the searchlight of the Holy Spirit
Begins to reveal me to *myself*
I so often close my eyes and turn my back
In a frantic but impossible effort
To escape Your penetrating gaze.
What a staggering contradiction, Lord
What appalling hypocrisy.
Apart from Your grace I am utterly shattered.
I ask You to sweep through me
Purify me, cleanse me completely.
From the depth of my penitent heart
I thank You for Your continual assurance
As I turn toward Your splintered cross:
Because of Your love I *became* our child
Because of Your grace I *remain* Your child.

New Bible

This was an exciting day for me, Lord!
This morning I opened my new Bible.
Not a single word was circled
Not a single phrase underlined.
Now with each new day
I can circle and underline again
I can word-clutter the margins
And I know what will happen, Lord—
I'll be asking as I read
Why didn't I see that before?
But even with the joy of a new Bible
I'm going to miss my old one
With its tattered pages—
Its creased and torn edges.
Oh; how many personal notes
Are jotted on the margins
How many God-whispered secrets.
Yes, Lord, I'll miss it.
But thank You for a friend's reminder:
"If your Bible is falling apart
Chances are your life isn't."

I Will Be Pleased

Lord, this fresh early morning
As I sit in our quiet living room
You've just reminded me
Through David the Psalmist
That there is incomparable joy
For those who delight to please You—
For those who are thinking about ways
To follow You more closely.
Lord, the day stretches out before me.
In a few brief moments I must arouse my family
And face again the noise, the distraction
The hubbub of confusion.
But while we are still alone
Just the two of us, Lord
While Your peace floods my tranquil heart
Please tell me what I can do
This duty-packed day
To follow You more closely.

Dearly loved child
Praise me joyfully
Talk with me intimately
Trust me totally
And I will be pleased.

Two Beautiful Parents

O dear Lord
I can never sufficiently thank You
For two beautiful parents
Who loved me into loving You.
Who praised me
Corrected me
Forgave me
And unwaveringly believed in me.
Who nurtured me
Nursed me back to health
And unceasingly prayed for me.
Who laughed with me
Cried with me
Comforted me
Rejoiced with me.
I know You better
Far better, Lord
Because of their authentic lives.
Thank You!

Lord,
Make Me Aware

Lord, make me aware of...
Sunlight filtering through the trees
The song of the March wind
Crickets at twilight
Water splashing in soapsuds
Yellow daffodils in a crystal vase
Delicate china on pink mats
The aroma of fresh coffee
The first day of spring
Green peas and red beets
A dewdrop on a rose
Freckles on a grinning face
The longing in my husband's eyes.

I Will Let You

Early this morning, Lord
An hour or so before dawn
You whispered a secret
Within my trembling heart...

You said, "If you will let Me
I will make this seeming tragedy
The most valuable experience
Of your entire life.
I will blaze a luminous trail
Through the vast wilderness.
Where there is sand and tumbleweed
I will cultivate a fertile valley.
I will plant green trees by still waters
If you will let Me."

O Lord, Yes!
I will let You!

You Dreamed
Me Up

O dear God
It was You, You alone
Who dreamed me up.
Nobody else
Would ever have thought of me
Or planned for me
Or looked right through me
With future contemplation.
Right from the beginning of time
I was all your idea.
You had big things in mind for me
Good things, glorious things
And now, with magnificent dexterity
You are making them come to pass.
And I?
Well, I stand amazed on the sideline
And praise Your infinite patience.

The Truant

Lord
What do You do with a truant
Who plays hooky from her Heavenly Parent?
What are the options?
One thing certain, You don't turn her off—
She's too noisy.
You don't pamper her because You know
She needs to stretch her spiritual muscles.
You don't shout, "Get up, foolish child"
Because she's covered with thick mud
From head to feet.
You don't condemn her because You said
"There is therefore now no condemnation..."

So in the end You do for her
What You always do for any bewildered
Half-demolished child of Yours:
You unlock her handcuffed spirit
With Your key of infinite love.
You check her fluctuating heart
With its spiritual irregularity.
When heart-to-heart resuscitation
Begins to revive her
You give her a fleeting glimpse
Of things as they could be.
Suddenly she knows with fresh gladness
That her one safe fortress
Is the center of Your will.
At least so it is with one truant...
Me.

Lord, Don't You Love Me Anymore?

Three
Unalterable Truths

Lord, through the years
Of walking hand-in-hand with You
I have learned three unalterable truths:
First, what You command me to do
You consistently expect me to do.
Never do You say, "Give the command a fair try."
Nor do You say, "Consider and then decide."
My natural weakness is never
An acceptable excuse.
Nor is my inability
To reach unreachable standards.
Rather, You tell me to *seek*
And then to *keep* Your commands.
Second, all of Your commands
Are always for my ultimate good.
"Obey Me," Your Word says
"So that I can do for you
All the wonderful things I promised..."
"In the keeping of My Word
There is great reward."
Third, whatever You command me to do
You fully enable me to do.
As You give light to reveal a command
So You give grace to fulfill it.
Your divine energy is always at my disposal.
The choice to obey is always mine.
The power to obey is always yours.

Everlasting Love

He is seven years old
And he's my friend.
His eyes are merry, his hair is short
His nose is covered with freckles.
On a cold, rainy day we sat on the floor
Eating hot buttered popcorn.
The popcorn went down quickly,
But the questions came slowly.

"If I told a lie today, would God stop loving me?"
"No, of course not, David."
"What if I told two lies, or three?
Would He stop loving me then?"
"No, but you'd be unhappy in your heart."
"What if I punched Johnnie in the nose
And made his nose bleed—*hard*?
Would God stop loving me then?"
"No, but you better not try it."
"What if I threw a rock and broke your window?
Would God stop loving me then?"
"No, but you'd have to work hard to pay for it."
"What if I stepped on the snails
That ate all your flowers?
Would God stop loving me then?"
"Not for a minute, David."
"When would God ever stop loving me?"
"David, not until there is no more earth
And no more heaven."

The Calendar

God, there are some years
We would like to cross off the calendar.
This is one of those years.
From January to December my husband and I
Have felt like wounded soldiers
Fighting a losing battle.
Hospitals, life-threatening illness
Surgeries, financial drain, pain
A family death, grief, anxiety
Night-tossing, weariness, silent tears.
Other things, too:
A flooded patio, pieces of roofing
Scattered by howling winds
Two car accidents in bumper-to-bumper traffic
Dwindling hope, thundering doubts
The fear-stabbing question
"Lord, don't You love us anymore?"

And yet, dear God
How dare we deny Your day-by-day comfort
At times when we needed it most.
Phone calls bringing encouragement, notes in the
mail
Delicious meals lovingly prepared by friends
A paragraph in a book renewing our trust
Your Word bringing light in the darkness
A sparrow's song during drizzling rain
Your whispered words to our hearts:
"When the pain stays, I stay, too."

O God, You have been our high tower
You have been our hiding place
You have been our sure defense.
The hymn of the Psalmist is our hymn, too:
"I will bless the holy Name of God
And not forget the glorious things He does."
Over this year's calendar we will finally write
"Surely the Lord was in this place
Though we knew it not."

The Living God

I place my whole confidence
In the Living God.
Not because things
Are going my way.
Not because I have what I want.
Not because I understand
All the inexplainables
Or because I am immune
To problems and pain and sorrow.
But despite my questions
My reversals, my disappointments
Despite my sorrow and tears
I place my whole confidence
In the Living God
For He alone can see me through.
He alone is worthy of my trust.

Beautiful
Things Happen

O God
Such beautiful things happen
When I meet You day by day
In quietness and confidence.
There is a deep inner wholeness
And the assurance of Your guidance.
I am not so easily disturbed
By changing circumstances.
I am less dependent on others
And more dependent on You.
My eyes may be full of tears
But my heart is full of joy.
In discovering Your hidden treasures
I learn how deeply I am treasured by You.
When day by day I am responsive
To Your whispered secrets
You do more for me in one day
Than I could do for myself in a lifetime.

Always There

So often, Lord
I reach the bottom of the abyss.
So often I taste the dregs
Of my own helplessness.
Yet it is there, *exactly there*
That You come to my immediate rescue.
When I feel totally impoverished
Of all self-sufficiency
When I want to vanish into nowhere
Form the depths of despair
I call Your Name
And You are always there for me!

Irreversible Yes

God, You have done
A beautiful thing for me.
You have freed me from the dissatisfaction
Of so many empty days and months.
Into my impoverished heart
You have poured life-changing thoughts of You
Making each new day gloriously rich.
You have struck a deep artesian well in my soul
As sheer joy springs forth.
All because in an act of honest surrender
When life had lost its challenge
I said an irreversible YES to You!

The Promise

God, on a long, lonely Saturday
Just before New Year's Day
You spoke so clearly through Your Word:
"Your days of mourning all will end.
You will live in joy and peace."
O God, what a glorious promise
As we begin a brand new year!
Again You said:
"Always be expecting much
From Him, your God."
I trust You implicitly, my Lord
For your "much" exceeds by far
My greatest comprehension of much.
Surely You have planned a beautiful surprise!
I open my heart wide to receive it.

What's Wrong, Lord

I am alone, Lord
So alone.
You no longer walk with me.
Or am I not walking with You?
Truly, I don't know.
However it is
I'm frightened, troubled, baffled.
Everything I do
Is with such fierce effort.
All my emotions are wire-crossed.
When others laugh, I cry.
When others run, I stumble.
When others sleep, I lie in darkness
Counting minutes, then hours.
I reach for Your hand
Until my fingers grow numb
Buy You give no response.
What's wrong, Lord?
How have I failed?
Don't You love me anymore?

Like A Lonely Tree

O God
On this cold January morning
I am like a lonely tree
On a distant mountaintop—
Leafless, brittle, trembling.
Howling winds twist me mercilessly.
How long must I wait, dear Lord
For the brilliant sun
To melt the heavy-packed snow?
And when will You prove
To my aching heart
That one lonely tree
On top of a snow-covered mountain
Has purpose wherever it grows!
As I stand against the forceful elements
I pray. I watch. I wait.
I long to see streams of water
Flowing down soft, rolling hills.
Perhaps I shall be productive again
When the long, long winter is past.

At Such Times

God, there are times
In the midst of heartache and heartbreak
When there is no comfort, no solace
Anywhere at all.
There are times
When in my crumbling state of mind
I feel I can no longer endure—
Not for a day, not even an hour.
It is at such times, O God
That I draw heavily
Upon Your unfathomable love.
At such times I implore
Your transforming peace.
At such times I live
By the power and promises
Of a Father who cares infinitely more
Than I can begin to grasp or comprehend.
Today, dear God, is a "such time."

By You, Dear God

To be tattered and torn
Bit by bit, day-in, day-out
Or to be shattered totally
Like a crystal goblet
Flung fiercely against a giant rock.
To know the brutal intensity
Of pain and despair.
O God
How unbearable it seems
How intolerable as it happens.

But finally, finally
To stand against the storm
To stretch with the strain
To accept the pain
With a measure of quiet hope.
To look beyond the intrusion
And above the confusion
To catch a glimpse of rainbow
In an ocean of tears...

O great God
This is to trace at last
Your guiding hand—
To sense Your gentle touch.
This is to know Your presence—
More precious than understanding—
To know Your compassion
Persists through the darkest night.

This is to walk courageously on
In the midst of a desolate wilderness.
This is to be loved
To be held
To be kept
By the Sustainer of the universe.

To be loved
To be held
To be kept
By You, dear God
By You!

Give Us a Token

Lord, today as I sit quietly
By my husband's hospital bed
All the rooms of my heart
Hold nothing but dark closets—
Musty and air-tight.
Please open another door
Or build another room in my heart
With wide-open windows
So I can glimpse the blue sky
Smell the fragrances of spring
And hear at least one chirping bird—
A token, dear Lord
That Your love is never-ending
Even when we're tempted to ask
"Don't You love us anymore?"

Lost Argument

I read this morning
Your direct and piercing question
To the ancient Job:
"Do you still want to argue
With the Almighty?
Or will you yield?"
With thoughtful heart
I read Job's wise reply:
"I am nothing...
How could I find the answers?
I lay my hand upon my mouth in silence."
You know so well what I do, God.
I continue to argue with You
As though I were in charge.
As though I could solve my own dilemma.
Finally in the end, broken and defeated
I yield to You, and then—peace.
Forgive me, dear God
For so foolishly ending
Where I should have begun.

I Needed this Experience

O God
This year has been so difficult
So humiliating and painful.
Not only have I failed
I have *utterly* failed.
How confident I felt at the beginning!
I was so sure of financial success.
I was so sure of praise and commendation.
But all that has come
From my self-implemented project
Is loss and rejection.

And yet, dear Lord
You knew so much better than I
That I needed this experience
To show me my gross indifference toward You.
I was not asking for wisdom
Or seeking Your help in making decisions.
I was manipulative, evasive, arrogant
Glued to the center of my own little world.
Then everything crashed around me
And I began to discover afresh, dear God
That no success in all the world
No glamour, no glitter
Can even begin to compensate
For not having You.

Relentless

God, You are relentless.
I have yielded
Everything to You—
Everything but one small exception—
An exception so small
I'm truly amazed
You would even take notice.
Yet it is invariably
To that one small exception
That You keep bringing me
Back, and back, and back.
Why does it matter so much to You?

My child
Why does it matter so much to you?

Please Teach
Me Well

God, it is drastically important
That the pain of this past year
Is not wasted.
How tragic it would be
To suffer so much
And gain so little.
What I *must* learn in my pain
Is that it is always leading
To something far beyond
What I can see in the shadows.
I *must* learn that You are not reckless
Or careless or cruel.
You are *for* me, and always
In some way, at some time
There is Your "nevertheless afterward."
I *must* learn that there is never a moment
When You are not worthy of praise.
Bad things happen
But there is only goodness in You.
I *must* learn that when my heart is broken
You are able to break my impatience, my pride
My carelessness and selfishness.
All of this I *must* learn.
O God, teach me well...teach me well.
It is drastically important
That the pain is not wasted.

In a Supermarket

Lord
While making my grocery list today
I suddenly began to wonder
If there was any possible way
I could serve You in a supermarket
Crowded with weary, stressful shoppers.
I seemed to hear You whisper
"A hundred lonely people need your smile."
Now as I hurriedly restock my shelves
After two hours of heavy shopping
I remember Your conservative estimate.
Surely I smiled more than a hundred times!
Thank You, Lord, for showing me
How to serve You in a supermarket
While pushing a cart loaded with groceries.

Frustration to Peace

Everything went wrong today—
Just everything.
Big things, little things
So many unforeseen problems
So many unanticipated demands.
My carefully planned agenda
Was so splattered with interruptions
I could scarcely read what I'd written.
Even before the end of the day
I was stricken with total fatigue.
The whole day was a nuisance
With very few moments of calm.
But just a little while before dinner
As I stood in the kitchen grating carrots
I suddenly felt my husband's gentle touch.
He turned me around and held me close.
Then very tenderly he took my hand
And placed it into the hand of God.
Suddenly a beautiful thing happened:
All my fruitless frustration
Turned to quiet peace.
Lord, thank You. Thank You so much!

Lost Shepherd

Sometimes, Lord
In my groping effort to find You
I have reversed the parable
Of the Shepherd and the sheep.
In my distorted concept
The Shepherd has been lost
And the sheep have trudged down
Dangerous mountain cliffs to find him.
How sadly prone I am to forget
That I would not be searching for You
If You were not first wanting me.
Let me remember always, Lord
How foolish it is
To stumble through darkness
Searching for You
When I need only to surrender
To Your search for me.

God, Why
Do You Hide

O God
Why do You hide from me
When I need You so much?
Why do You make it so difficult
For me to find You
When I know You are there?
When You have given me
Great and glorious promises
Why are none of them fulfilled?
When loneliness overwhelms me
Where is Your hand?
When I am depleted with fatigue
Where is Your rest?
O God, why do You hide from me?

Child of many questions
How can I answer
When you never stop asking?

Time To Act

Lord
Today You clearly told me
To get on with the job—
The task I've been evading
The task You've told me
Countless times to tackle.
You reminded me forcefully
That I've been praying long enough.
It's time now to ACT!
As I obey You will reward me
With peace and spiritual prosperity.
Again I see that obedience
Is always the thing with You.

My Destiny

O God
Despite my deep desire to please You
In the midst of confinement and pain
There are so many temptations
That hover like a thick cloud
Over all my honest efforts.
Is there ever an escape, dear God
From the subtle temptations
That accompany perpetual pain?
How can I avoid the clamoring thoughts
The weakness, the helplessness
The pricking irritations?
Then, dear God, there are the weary mornings
After sleepless nights.
The disturbing fears that cling so tightly.
How can I resist the "if onlys"
When the pain pierces with such intensity?

Over and over the question Why? creeps stealthily
Into the dark corners of my thoughts.
"Why *this*, dear God, when I long to serve You?"
"Why *this*, when in an instant You could make
me well?"
And yet, dear God, I know I must stop brooding.
I must stop badgering.
You need not explain Your eternal purpose
In terms I can understand.

Help me to respond without murmuring
About Your method of molding me
For I can know with unshakable assurance
That my destiny is perfection
In the eternal presence of the living God.

How Long Is Everlasting

O dear God
How long will You ignore me?
How long must I continue to weep before You?
Will You forever keep silent
When I seek Your face?
Surely You know my desperation
And yet I cannot arouse Your attention.
Must I continually stumble
Through dense forests and dark valleys?
Does it matter to You about me?
I don't understand, Lord.
In the past You so lavishly blessed me.
Have I offended You?
Are there false motives that I cannot trace?
Are You searching me out?
O Lord, I cannot endure the thought
That You no longer love me.
Hear my cry, dear God.
Please speak to me.

Listen, dear child
Quietly listen.
I have loved you
With an everlasting love.
How long is everlasting?

Descendant of Adam

Lord, at times of soaring victory
The Psalmist said he would sing to You
As long as he lived.
He said he would praise You
To his very last breath.
He said he would bless Your Name forever.
But, Lord, how well I remember
David's bitter complaints
During days of fear and despair.
He asked if You had forgotten to be gracious.
He asked if he had offended You.
He asked if Your mercy was gone forever.
As you forgave David's complaints
Lord, please forgive mine.
I too am a descendant of Adam!

God of All Grace

God of all grace
Please bring an end
To this hideous nightmare.
Lift the heavy weight of despondency.
Remove the confusion
The brokenness
The crushing anxiety
The awful pain.
How I long to sense the joy
Of Your healing touch.
You are a God of integrity
A God of infinite kindness
Surely it cannot be true
That You no longer love me.

Wrong Question

My faithful God
I see afresh this morning
The grave error of my question
"Don't You love me anymore?"
I ought always to ask instead
"How can You love me so continually
With such immeasurable love?"

The Promise

(2 SAMUEL 22:29, TLB)

And the Lord will lighten my darkness...

O Lord, how I needed to read this promise
In Your Word this very day.
You will lighten my darkness.
You will *personally* do it.
I cannot, nor can my family.
My friends cannot
Nor can the one dearest to me.
You alone can lighten my darkness.
Though it is pitch black
Though clouds pile heavy and high
Though thunder roars
Though I see only confusion
You will lighten my darkness.
My hope is in You.
I look for You. I wait for You.
Nothing will prevent it.
You will lighten my darkness.

You Promised Me

Lord, just today I read again
The words of the prophet, Ezra.
Long years ago he prayed
"You have done what You promised
For You are always true to Your word."
My dear Lord, look into my heart.
Listen to my repeated plea.
You promised me, Lord
You promised me.
You promised deliverance
From crushing defeat.
You promised Your peace
In my aching despair.
You promised release
From agonizing pain.
I've waited so long...so long.
Still I cling tenaciously
To this solemn truth:
You are always true to Your word.
I trust You, dear God.
I expect to pray as Ezra prayed:
"You have done what You promised
For You are always true to Your word."

Day of Rejoicing

Lord, all day long
We've been laughing and singing.
We've been shouting and praising.
After weeks and months
Of waiting and pleading
You have wonderfully answered our prayers.
Our hearts are filled with unspeakable joy.
You promised that those
Who sow in tears
Shall reap in joy.
It is happening, dear Lord
To us...to *us!*

Immediately

Dear Lord
I'm so tired of living
In my little cramped vessel—
So weary of dangling my feet in the water
But never stepping out of the boat.
I want to walk the waves with You
Just as Peter did.
True, he took only a few steps
Before losing his courage
But at least he was heading toward You.
Lord, I'm coming, too!
If I begin to falter or sink
I trust You to catch me
Just as You caught Peter.
Remember, Lord?
You caught him *immediately*.

Free Choice

My Lord
Because You have given me
The irrevocable power of free choice
You will not force me
To do something
I selfishly don't want to do.
But I have made
A grave and painful discovery:
You can certainly
Make me wish I had done it.

Soul Struggle

Her uncontrollable sobs know no respite.
"What is wrong with me"
She stammers convulsively
"That love has passed me by?
Am I so ugly, so stupidly plain?
Am I some kind of an oddity?
Doesn't God love me anymore?"

Lord, there are times when she hides
Behind a sophisticated facade
But today she is not pretending.
In her deep loneliness
There are no words to comfort her.
You alone can release her
From her shadowy world.
You alone can break the bleakness
And produce the firm conviction
Of Your measureless love.
Lord, my part in her soul's struggle
Is to reach for her hand.
Your part is to reach for her heart.

The Promise

O dear God, I continue to believe
Your personal promise still stands
Though every quivering emotion within
Shouts that it will be broken.
I am claiming Your help through the wilderness
Despite every frightening shadow and vale.
Often you do the most
When You seem to do the least.
Sometimes secretly
Sometimes quietly
Often slowly
But always most certainly
You are true to Your word.
And so, my Lord
Though I am weak, weary, and worn
Help me not to despair.
You see me, You hear me.
You know I am depending utterly
Upon Your unblemished integrity.
Surely You will keep Your word.

O God...My God

O God...*My* God
Though You now seem totally hidden
I am clinging to You hopefully
Even confidently.
Someday, some way, You will make
All You are now permitting
Blessedly clear.
With fixed purpose, dear God
I am determined to wait, to trust
To rely upon Your faithfulness.
Despite the drain and strain
I anticipate new perspectives
And fresh depths of insight
Into all that is now so mysterious.
O God, in ways unanticipated
You are teaching me the great truth
Of Samuel Rutherford's words:
"I see that grace grows best in winter."
Thank You, dear God
Thank You for that!

Watchman, What of the Night?

Today I read again
The piercing question
In the book of Isaiah:
"Watchman, what of the night?"
I too have asked a question, my Lord:
In the darkness of my nights
When pain permeates my body
When sleep evades me
When fatigue overwhelms me
When I cannot run or hide
Will You be my night watchman?
And when in fear and desperation
I ask, "Watchman, what of my night?"
Please let me hear Your gentle words:
"Joy cometh in the morning."

Undeniable Truth

God, forgive me.
I am suddenly aware
That for many months
I have been more occupied
With my personal pain and loss
Than I have been with You.
I know it is true:
You are not obligated to explain
My crushing blows or my aching void.
Help me to trust You for who You are
Regardless of what You permit.
I acknowledge Your Sovereignty, God
But I long for You to burn
Into every fiber of my being
The undeniable truth
That throughout all eternity
You are a loving, caring
And forever faithful Sovereign.

Wistful Longing

O God
Where is the strong assurance
I knew so well a short time ago?
Why is my heart suddenly so empty
And my thoughts so dull?
Why am I tormented with pain
And tortured with doubt?
What has corroded my trust?
Please, dear Lord
In Your loving-kindness
Break into my cloud of confusion
And free me as You would have done
Had I touched the hem of Your garment
When You walked on earth.
I look to You with wistful longing.
I wait for Your gentle touch.

Overwhelmed

Lord, I'm overwhelmed
By my inadequacies and failures.
So often I'm ashamed
To face my friends.
I continually sense
That they look down on me.
It's my greatest problem.

Foolish child
Your greatest problem
Is that you don't
Look up to Me.

Sudden Awe

My face wind-lashed
With stinging sand
Alone I trudge the beach
Filled with sudden awe
That You, O God
Are mightier by far
Than all the breakers
Pounding on the seashores
Of the world.

"Great Stirrer-Up"

Lord, Frank Laubach was right
When he spoke of You
As the "Great Stirrer-Up."
Invariably You are determined
To stir me out of my lethargy
And self-satisfaction.
When once again You have aroused me
And restored my sensitivity
To the plan You have ordained for me
You amaze me with delightful surprises
I would never have discovered on my own—
Never in a thousand years!
What a true description of You, God—
The "Great Stirrer-Up."

A Beautiful Word

O God, our quarrel this early morning
Was so senseless, so demolishing.
We slashed each other with sarcasm.
We said cruel things to each other—
Things we honestly didn't mean.
I know I am far too sensitive, Lord.
Touchy might be a more accurate word.
My inclination is always first to brood
And then to inflict the silent treatment
Waiting for my husband to make amends.

But when I think of our solid marriage
Of forty-three productive years
One truth is deeply ingrained within me:
There is no hurt worth clinging to
When we love each other as we do.
Lord, *forgiveness* is a beautiful word.
Tonight when my husband comes home from
work
May I be the first to forgive
The minute he unlocks the door.

I Trust You

Lord, it was on an April morning
So many years ago
That You said to me so clearly
"Trust Me and you won't be disappointed."
Having heard You on that special morning
I simply cannot "unhear" you now.
I can't forget that morning
Nor do I think You want me to.
Because You live in an eternal Now
Your words are just as relevant today
As they were that long-ago morning.
I *trust* You. You will not disappoint me!

Lonely Heart

O God
How I long to encourage her—
To say or do something
To renew her shattered hope.
She told me that when her husband left
You seemed to leave, too.
Panic seized her, and dread.
A sense of futility.
"If God is a God of love," she sobbed
"How could He let this happen?"
Despairing, she trudges
Through each dreary day
Too unsure to start afresh
Too confused right now to pray.
Lord, create within her
A deep longing for You.
If she turns form You
As her husband turned from her
She will be twice bereft.
God, I will walk with her
On her winding journey toward recovery
But You alone can heal her empty heart.

The Great Investment

I praise You, dear Lord
For teaching my husband and me
To make friends with the money
You have entrusted to us.
We have so little to invest
In stocks and bonds
But so much to invest
In lonely, empty lives.
And, Lord, the rate of interest
Is enormously high.
In fact, as we continue to invest
The interest goes up and up and up!

Welcome Home

Dear lonely old man!
Just a bit eccentric, perhaps.
Friendly whenever he had a chance to be
But certainly nobody thought he was stimulating.
When he walked he was always alone.
In church he sat alone, too.
Always near the rear of the sanctuary.
That's why I was so surprised
To see so many at his memorial service.
Some who would not have crossed the street
To greet him while he still lived.
Lord, he must have loved his entrance to heaven.
Never before had anyone stood in line
Just to welcome him home!

Hurting Heart

How pathetically she attempts
To be courageous and strong
Despite her desperate need
To express her deep grief.
She solemnly promised her husband
She would stand firm
When his death parted them.
She said, "I want to keep my promise.
He would trust me to do that."
And so she smiles while her lips quiver—
And her longing heart weeps.
Soon, perhaps, the pushed-back tears will come.
I pray so, Lord. Oh, I pray so!
But right now, please hold her hurting heart
As a mother holds a hurting child.

Indictment

O God
When I think of Your
Tremendous goodness to us
Your continual poured-out blessings
Suddenly I am overwhelmed
With a convicting thought:
Everything You do
For my husband and me
All Your love and kindness
So lavishly bestowed
Become an indictment
Unless we willingly
Allow each blessing
To flow through us to others.
All Your abundance
Must constantly be on the move
Or we will stagnate
In a sea of plenty.

Forgive My Critical Attitude

Lord
Forgive my critical attitude—
My judgmental spirit.
It is true that I saw my friend fall again
But not once did I consider
The countless times she did *not* fall
Though she was severely tempted.
Help me to bind myself more closely
And more lovingly to her.
May she know that I continue to believe
In Your victory in her life
Despite any sudden barrier of defeat.
May I redouble my love and vigilance
Until she is renewed and restored—
Until she is able to give to others
The support she herself has received.

Thanksgiving
Day Dream

On this fragrant, frosty Thanksgiving Day
The huge turkey browns beautifully
In our king-size oven.
The tender yams are evenly candied;
The corn souffle is beginning to bubble;
The congealed salad is ready to unmold.
The homemade bread with its crunchy texture
Is wrapped in foil for reheating.
The ice cubes are bagged in plastic;
The relishes are artistically arranged
On a round crystal plate.
The pumpkin pies are still slightly warm.
Fresh yellow chrysanthemums
Grace the long, colorful table.
The house glistens and shines.
My makeup is evenly applied...

So, dear family
How about settling down
In our favorite chairs
For an hour of relaxation
Before our guests arrive!

Lord, I dream of this happening
Some ethereal Thanksgiving Day!

He's Late Again

Lord, he's late again.
It's raining so hard
And traffic is always heavy
At this time of day.
I never feel secure
With those huge trucks
On the freeway.
Could a tire have gone flat?
Did he stop to see someone?
Surely he would have called.
I wonder...didn't he feel well
When he left this morning?
I remember how gently he held me
When he kissed me good-bye.
Did he think something might happen?
When we prayed at the table
I asked You to keep him safe.
Did You hear me, Lord?
Dinner is getting cold.
Should I reheat the oven?
Wait! I think I hear the car door slam.
I do! Beautiful sound! He's home!

Why does he do this to me, Lord?
Doesn't he understand my stress?
Doesn't he stop to think
I could have a heart attack?

The Grief
You Endure

God, how can he fail You so unashamedly?
How can he disobey so excessively?
How can he turn his back on You
And blatantly continue his own defiant way?
How can he excuse his gross selfishness
His pride, his stubborn resistance?
How can he so totally ignore You
And pretend that all is well?
How my heart aches, dear God
For the grief You endure for him.

My troubled child
Does anyone ache for you?

Though It Takes a Lifetime

Lord—
Sometimes I wonder
How two imperfect people
Can possibly build
A perfect marriage.
And then I stop wondering
For I know they cannot.

But this they can do:
They can invite You
The perfect One
To share day by day
In their togetherness.
Gently, carefully
You will nurture them.
You will transform
Their imperfections.

Though it takes a lifetime
Their marriage will bear
Luscious fruit...like a tree
Planted along a riverbank—
And all that they do
Shall prosper.

Forty-Three Years

Forty-three years of marriage.
That's a lot of years!
Somewhere in a box of treasured things
I still have the postcard
I sent to my parents
While we were on our honeymoon.
I saved it because of its rare combination
Of humor and naïveté:
"Bliss! Nothing but bliss!
Day after day of uninterrupted bliss!"
That sentimental bit of melodrama
Was written after we had given our marriage
The long, enduring test of—eleven days.
We had a lot to learn!

One thing is certain:
Whatever marriage was meant to be
It wasn't meant to be easy.
It's different when you're married.
You're accountable to each other.

You're making a life investment
In a permanent relationship.
At least that was our personal decision
Right from the very beginning.
True, sometimes I'm plodding
When I'd rather soar.
Or I'm submerged in soapsuds
When I'd rather be sunning on a sandy shore.
But when it comes right down to it
I wouldn't trade my lot
With any woman who ever lived....

We lie side by side in the darkness.
Our fingers touch, our weary bodies relax.
Before we go to sleep my husband says
With beautiful gentleness
"I want you to know
I'm lying here loving you."

Forty-three years are a lot of years.
Lord, thank You for every one!

Marriage
Is So
Much
More,
Lord

Remind Them Gently

O Lord
Please talk to them—
This beautiful couple
Whose marriage is disintegrating.
God, they've known so much of beauty.
They've endured so much pain.
They've laughed together, wept together.
They've groped through appalling darkness
Upholding each other step by step.
They've suffered together, triumphed together.
They've planned and prayed together.
Now, dear God
Before it is too late
Remind them tenderly of Your command:
"What God has joined together
Let no man put asunder."
Before it is too late
Remind them gently, Lord
That two lives so intricately woven
Into a blended pattern
Can never be wholly separate lives again.

Shining Reward

O dear Lord
How unprepared we were
For the breathtaking surprises
Awaiting us in our marriage.
We simply didn't know
How much we didn't know.
We couldn't see
Every part of marriage.
But we knew we had promised
What we couldn't see.
It didn't take long to discover
That marriage wasn't the end of struggle.
All of a sudden it was just beginning.
But the one shining reward
Through the fleeting years is this:
While we've shared the struggles
We've doubled the joys!

Still More

I love you!
You are so uncluttered
So open to love and laughter and life.
There are no dark, musty corners in you
No cobwebbed crevices
Of hatred and hostility.
There are no rusty nails of bitterness
No dusty cabinets of prejudice and pretense.

I love you!
You weave within me a delicate pattern
Of wind and sea
Of sunlight and stars.
You soothe me, comfort me, release me.
You are like a quiet song.

I love you!
You are so willingly, so totally
Surrendered to God.
I know Him better because of you.

I love you!
When I awaken in the morning
I shall love you still more.

Baseball Season Again

One night on our honeymoon
I asked if you'd think of me
Every single minute
No matter where you were
Or what you were doing.
Do you remember, my love?

You laughed heartily.
Finally you said
"Do you mind if occasionally
I wonder who's winning
The World Series?"

That was years ago.
It's baseball season again.
And no...
I don't mind.

Our Tomorrows, Too

O dear God
The value of a promise
Depends upon the promiser.
You have promised
Never to leave us or forsake us.
You have promised
To make the crooked places straight.
You have brought us this far
In our years of marriage.
You have taken us through
Illness, loss, pressure, pain.
You will not let us down now.
It is impossible, dear God.
It would be inconsistent
With Your character.
You are our Father!
You are our Friend!
What You are now permitting
Must surely be for our ultimate good.
By Your enabling power
We refuse to let anxiety destroy us.
You have been in all our yesterdays
You will be in our tomorrows, too.

Suddenly We Knew

Suddenly we knew
We'd never be the same again...
Tonight we knelt by the side of our bed
Bruised, broken, bewildered
Hearts aching
Tears streaming
Torrents of fear
Saturating our very souls
Lost, lonely, imprisoned
Stricken with regret...
Please hear us, dear God!
Are You there?
Do You see?
Do You care?
Show us, shake us, remake us.

Then out of the desolate darkness
The clear witness of Your voice:
Behold, I make all things new.
Surrender...solace...joy!
Unspeakable joy!
O dear God, thank You!
Suddenly we knew
We'd never be the same again.

Sunday Morning

We sit in church together
Clasping hands so unobtrusively
That nobody else is aware.
We stand to sing the Doxology
And our fingers touch.
As we reverently bow our heads
In sacred, silent prayer
We both know we are thanking God
For a thousand precious gifts—
Including the gift of our love.
We give our tithes and offerings
With abundant gratitude.
We listen to an anthem of exaltation
And our hearts throb.
We are deeply challenged
By the message of the morning.
With renewed dedication we pray
"Lord, may we live what we have heard."
We rise for the benediction
And there is between us
A rare and precious closeness.
We greet the guests and members
To our right and to our left.
Their warm response rekindles love.
We leave the sanctuary together—
Husband and wife.
God, thank You for a meaningful hour
Of joyful worship and praise.

With Each
Passing Anniversary

Please, dear Lord
Protect us against the subtle hazards
That so often threaten a marriage.
We'd like to think after thirty years
That we've battled through it all.
We'd like to think that it's time
To wave banners
And blow bugles
And shout to the world
"We've arrived!"
But the simple fact is—
Our marriage can be thrown into a tailspin
Anytime along the way
Unless we continually explore new heights
Pursue new goals
And deepen our spiritual concepts.
Lord, help us to make our promises
And renew our vows
With deeper assurance than ever before.
May we never be too preoccupied
To respond to each other
Or too selfish to cooperate
Or too indifferent to compromise.
With each passing anniversary
May this be our joyful declaration:
Never have I loved you
As much as I love you now.

God of Promises

Lord, this very day
This very hour
My husband and I
Have come face to face
With a wrenching crisis.
Our work has folded
Our finances are depleted
Our ambitious plans have exploded
Our glistening dreams are smashed.
We don't know where to turn—
Or scarcely how to pray.
Yet, Your Word tells us
There is not a single catastrophe
No matter how staggering
No matter how shattering
That we may not bring to You.
It isn't only that we *may*—
You tell us that we *must*.

Dear God of the Promises
You are never lost in our mysteries.
Our eyes are turned toward You.
Keep us from looking back.
While we wait with bleeding hearts
Remind us again, and yet again
That our absence of happiness
Does not mean the absence of God.

April Day

O Lord
You've been so lavish
With Your paintbrush
This singing April day!
The whole world is vibrant
With the ecstasy of spring.
Our huge purple pansies
Are taking off like wild.
But I'm not surprised.
I'm sure my husband's
Gentle, patient care
Is part of the reason
For their delicate beauty.
If it works on pansies
As it works on me
No wonder they flourish!

A Beautiful Word

O dear Lord
Without Your forgiveness
Life would be intolerable
So futile and fearful
So filled with despair.
How could we endure the agonizing guilt
Of our mismanaged lives
Our deliberate wrong choices
Our gross selfishness
Our appalling inconsistencies!
How could we endure the memory
Of our raging anger
Our bitter words
Our lustful thoughts—
Thoughts we would never dare
Flash upon a public screen.
But there is forgiveness with You.
Total! Complete!
You remember our sins no more.
We can focus our thoughts on today.
We can joyfully anticipate
The possibilities of tomorrow.
There need be no gnawing guilt
No morbid introspection.
On the cross You took care of it all.
O dear Lord
Forgiveness is a beautiful word!

Waiting

"I waited patiently
For God to help me..."
The Psalmist said it centuries ago.
We are saying it today—
My husband and I.
Waiting!
How difficult it is.
Hoe disastrous it often seems.
Waiting when life is at a standstill
When nothing changes or moves
When the baffling problems intensify.
We pray...hope...plead
Through tedious days
Through restless nights
While God seems to walk out the door.
To wait patiently
Is like adding insult to injury.
Even the solutions we think might work
Crumble to worthless bits.
Yet, in the midst of fear and turmoil
We secretly recall the countless times
We've cringed with remorse
Over our lack of trust
After the glorious answer came.
O God
Help us to wait...
To wait patiently!

Squabbles

"Why do you always—"
"Hey, wait a minute—
I don't always..."
"You interrupted me.
How do you know
What I was going to say?"
"I don't know
But whatever it was
I don't *always.*"

"See, you *never* listen."
"Yes, I do!"
"When?"
"When you call dinner."

O dear Lord
The Creator of our lives
And of our marriage
Thank You for the spontaneous laughter
That so often resolves
Our stupid, childish squabbles.

Beginning To Recognize

God, we are beginning to recognize
The far-reaching implications
Of our marriage vow
Till death do us part.
Not tension of financial pressure
Or difficulties or sickness
Or emotional insecurity—but *death.*
We are beginning to recognize
That apart from Your enabling power
Our personal promises
Become passive and powerless.
We are beginning to recognize
That You are the Keeper of Promises—
That You alone can fortify ours.
God, You are more eager
To make us holy than happy
More eager to build character
Than continual contentment
More eager to make us conformable
To the Son of God
Than to the world about us.
We are beginning to recognize
That commitment is total
With never a thought of quitting.
We are beginning to recognize
That love is stronger than death—
That marriage is an incredible venture
Ordained and sanctioned by You!

The Devastation
of Boredom

God, help us at any cost
To avoid the danger of boredom.
How deadly it can be!
Teach us to stretch our imaginations
And release our whirling creativity.
Help us to excitedly exchange
Ideas, goals, dreams...
May we share freely
Our fears, wounds, anxieties...
May we laugh together—hilariously!
Keep us caring, genuinely caring!
May we never isolate each other
Or shut each other out.
Total agreement is not so essential.
We needn't always pursue the same hobbies.
Or share the same political views.
But help us, God
To be eagerly interested
In each other's opinions
In each other's convictions.
May we believe in each other
Congratulate each other
Share secrets together.
Have crazy fun together.
May we share everything with You!
Shield us, dear God
From the devastation of boredom!

Forever

Sometimes, my dear
I want to ask:
Why do you love me?
When did you first love me?
Are you sure you love me?
Do you ever not love me?
Do you love me more than yesterday?
Will you love me more tomorrow?
Will you love me a year from today?
Ten years from today?
Do you love me every morning?
Do you love me when you're asleep?
And then suddenly
All my questions seem foolish
And childishly immature.
I know that you love me
You know that I love you
And "love goes on forever."

Marriage

Marriage!
It's rough. It's tough. It's work.
Anybody who says it isn't
Has never been married.
Marriage has far bigger problems
Than toothpaste squeezed
From the middle of the tube.

Marriage means...
Grappling, aching, struggling.
It means putting up
With personality weaknesses
Accepting criticism
And giving each other freedom to fail.
It means sharing deep feelings
About fear and rejection.
It means turning self-pity into laughter
And taking a walk to gain control.

Marriage means...
Gentleness and joy
Toughness and fortitude
Fairness and forgiveness
And a walloping amount of sacrifice.

Marriage means...
Learning when to say nothing
When to keep talking
When to push a little
When to back off.
It means acknowledging
"I can't be God to you—
I need Him, too."

Marriage means...
You are the other part of me
I am the other part of you.
We'll work through
With never a thought of walking out.

Marriage means...
Two imperfect mates
Building permanently
Giving totally
In partnership with a perfect God.
Marriage, my love, means us!

I Love Being Married to You

I love the little things you do...
Like opening the car door
And placing my chair at the table
And grabbing my hand at a party.

I love the humorous things you do...
Like leaving three M & Ms
On the breakfast bar
With a note which says
"No matter how you arrange the colors
They still say I love you."

I love the ridiculous things you do...
Like hiding my gown
When I'm ready for bed.

I love the happy things you do...
Like whistling cheerfully
While you're trimming the hedge
In our backyard.

I love the thoughtful things you do...
Like fixing the breakfast coffee
And keeping the car gassed
And always remembering
Birthdays and anniversaries.

I love the significant things you do...
Like providing ample insurance
And updating our will
And arranging a neat list
Of important telephone numbers.

I love the magnificent things you do...
Like sharing God's Word
And pledging to pray for me
Every day of your life.

To put it precisely, dear darling
I love being married to you!

A Better Way

My love...I remember
The day I said to you
So defensively, so decisively
"That's just my way of doing things.
You'll have to get used to me!"
After you left for your office
God said to me
So pointedly, so pertinently
Why don't you settle
For MY way of doing things?
You'll be much more fun to live with!

Without a
Single Word

So often you say *I love you*
Without a single word...
When you reach for my hand
In the silent darkness
When you leave a love note
On the kitchen sink
When you empty the trash—
The task you most dislike
When you fold the laundry
Just to surprise me
When you make a special trip
For my favorite candy bar
When you awaken me in the morning
With a cup of steaming coffee
When you wink across the table
As we're entertaining guests
When you rub my aching shoulders
While I'm sitting at my desk
When you walk through the door
With a single long-stemmed rose
And a card that says
Just-Because Day...
When someone asks
"Does your husband say he loves you?"
My answer is always the same—
"At least a thousand times a day."

Are We Compatible?

We sit here quietly
In our peaceful living room
With a cup of fresh coffee.
I page through a current magazine.
I read, "Do you have a happy marriage?
Are you and your husband compatible?"

Well, I always thought so, darling
But let's see...
I'm always late; you're always early
I'm noisy, demonstrative; you're often quiet.
I adore love songs; you prefer symphonies.
I go for details; you want the highlights.
I like to soak in the bathtub; you prefer a shower.
My closet is almost always organized.
Yours is almost always cluttered.

How disillusioning!
After all our married years
We suddenly discover we're incompatible.
But wait—let's not panic.
There's still the other side of the coin:
We love walking together in the drizzling rain
And hiking over hills on a crisp November day.
We love eating apples before an open hearth
And reading aloud to each other.
We love picnics and barbecues
And watermelon in July.

We love laughing and sharing
And singing and praying.
We love eating ice cream in bed
And whispering secrets in the darkness.
So—does it balance out, darling?
Shall we keep it going a little longer?
Are we compatible?

A Long Way to Go

Sometimes, my love
When I look back
To our early beginning
I wonder why in the world
God chose me for you.
I was so often unloving, unkind
Sometimes just plain obstinate—
Remember?
I don't mean I'm suddenly perfect
Or that after all our years together
I've gloriously arrived.
God would be the first to say
I've got a long way to go!
But at least I begin to appreciate
How wonderfully creative love is.
You didn't wait for me
To become worthy of love.
In your gentle, consistent
Sometimes stubborn way
You just kept on loving me
Until I began to feel whole.
Out of the wholeness came the changes
God was so eager, so willing to make.
He's not finished yet!

The Things
You Never Do

Thank you for the things
You never do:
You never embarrass me
With crude, uncouth remarks
You never criticize me
In the presence of others
You never downgrade
My personal achievements.
You never compete with me
You never compare me unfavorably
With other wives
You never make me feel
Unnecessary or unneeded.
You never hide behind a newspaper
While we're eating together
You never refuse to hear me out
In a controversial discussion.
You never remind me of past mistakes
You never rule with an iron rod
You never treat my parents unkindly.
You never degrade me
You never betray me
You never deluge me with
I-told-you-so's
You never go to sleep
Without kissing me good-night.

I Love To
Introduce You

I love to introduce you
As my husband in a mingling crowd.
I love your firm handclasp
Your smiling eyes, your genuine laugh.
I'm proud to stand by your side
When you say with honest enthusiasm
"It's a pleasure to meet you!"
I like the way you put guests at ease
The way you center in on them.
I like the questions you ask—
Pertinent and direct—
To show your interest and concern.
I never feel stranded when we're together.
You are never neglectful.
I never have to turn to someone else
For response or support.
You make me feel confident and content
And always very sure of your love.
I look at other couples.
I listen, I smile, I share
But my heart always turns toward you.
Even in a crowd
The longer we're together
The more I learn of love.

A Thousand Years

A thousand years from tonight
It won't make the slightest difference.
That's what I've been telling myself
For the past sleepless hour.
But tonight...right now
It makes all the difference in the world
That I am in *this* bed
And you are in *that* bed
And we are a thousand miles apart
Right here in the same small house.

I can't stand it another minute!
I'm about to make the fastest
Thousand-mile journey
In the history of world travel.
Please move over, darling—
I know you're not asleep.
I've come to tell you
It was mostly my fault
And I'm very, very sorry...
Even though a thousand years from tonight
It won't make the slightest difference.

Habitual Reminders

I'm driving you to work this morning.
Of course, your reminders are habitual:
"Better slow down a little, honey."
"A car to your right—do you see it?"
"Better change lanes—
The next off-ramp is ours..."

Sometimes, dear darling
I wonder how I ever managed
To pass the driver's test
And renew my license
Before I married you!

Right Now

....

I need you *right now!*
Not an hour from now
When you've finished reading the paper.
Not after dinner when the dishes are done
And we settle down for an hour of television.
Not when we turn out the lights
And sleepily say good-night
But right now.

I need your arms around me
Sheltering, protecting, comforting.
I need your encouragement
Even though I've pulled some blunders
And made some stupid decisions today.
I need your heart applause
And your special brand of tenderness.
I'm sure you know, dear love
That for the most part
I try not to burden you
With a long list of petty complaints
The minute you walk through the door.
But once in awhile (like now)
I need your touch, your closeness
Even if
I must stumble over your coffee mug
Sit on the arm of your chair
Interrupt your reading
And say so right now.
The beautiful thing is—it works!
You're with me right now.

Morning Love Note

This, my dear husband
Is the love note
You slipped under my coffee cup
One early sunlit morning...

"How I thank God for you
And your beautiful love.
He is so good to have given me you!
In all the changing scenes of each day
Regardless of pressures, tensions
And unexpected emergencies
There is always the beautiful stability
Of your devoted love for me
And His everlasting love for us both...
I pray this will be a happy day for you!
Surrender it to His will.
He is working a miracle in you
To give you an undreamed-of victory.
Regardless of feelings or seemings
God is in control!
Today is another day to experience His joy!
I love you all there is...."

O dear God
Thank You for speaking
So clearly
So dearly
Through the husband I love.

Do You Remember?

First you forgot your car keys
Then your briefcase.
You drove around the block
And thought of your checkbook.
When I heard the door open
The fourth time, I asked,
"What now, honey?"
"Just my glasses," you said casually.
You hugged me and added
"I'll see you at dinnertime."
I said, "I'll see you in five minutes."
And I did!
Do you remember, my love?

I Will Wait for You

Right now, my love
I would like to know
What you are thinking
What you are feeling.
This very moment
I know you are hurting deeply.
Your eyes always give you away.
But if for one reason
Or many reasons
You cannot tell me now
If words don't come easily
If somehow you are reluctant
To unlock the door of your heart
Please know I am with you
Just the same.
I will wait for you
With patience and understanding
Because I love you
With all there is of me.

Just for Today

Lord, too often my morning prayer
Is merely a monologue.
I bombard You with my needs.
I push upon You my self-made plans.
Then I discourteously hurry off
To do my own thing
In my own haphazard way.

But today it's different, Lord.
Today I wait quietly in Your presence.
I give You my full attention
As I wait Your timetable.
Help me all day to detect Your nudges
Your inner promptings.
Prepare me for the interruptions
That are bound to come.
Dispel the negative thoughts
That creep in so subtly—
And fill my heart with music!

So Much To Learn

Two months before our wedding...
    I explained it ever so carefully.
    With exaggerated emphasis I said
    "In my family my brothers or my father
    ALWAYS empty the wastebaskets."

Two months after our wedding...
    I stood in our cheerful kitchen
    Glaring defiantly
    At the bright yellow wastebasket
    With its overflowing contents.
    I glanced at the accumulated scraps
    Scattered on the floor.
    With mounting antagonism, I thought
    In my family my brothers or my father
    ALWAYS emptied the wastebaskets.
    I was all alone in our apartment.
    Suddenly I gasped when out of nowhere
    I distinctly heard:
    You have two hands and two feet.
    Hum a little tune, empty the basket
    And remember how frequently
    Your husband dries the dishes for you.

Today...
> O Lord
> The immensity of marriage
> Often overwhelms me!
> There is always so much to learn.
> Big things...little things
> Simple things...complicated things.
> Sometimes we learn
> In spite of our differences.
> More often we learn because of them.

Reflections

It's a funny thing...
You can think about marriage
Dream about it
Talk about it
You can even take all kinds
Of marriage preparation courses.
But when it really happens to you
Suddenly you discover
You don't know nearly as much
As you thought you did.
At times you succeed.
At other times you take a spill
And have to pull each other up.
Maturity doesn't suddenly drop in
Like an unexpected gust of March wind.
You have to grow into it
Slowly...steadily...
Sometimes painfully.
And often it's the pain
That makes us love each other more.

You Said So

O God
Thank You!
I am not a catastrophe
Or a morbid mistake.
I am not an afterthought
Or a no-purpose being.
I am not a comedy of errors.
I am not bad news.
I am not minimal.
I am not redundant.
I am not a little cog
In a huge machine....

I am irreplaceable!
I am the product
Of the Holy Trinity
Created to be made complete.
When anyone has done for me
What You have done
I'm not about to be forgotten.
To You, dear God
I have infinite, eternal value.
You've chosen me
To be Your very own.
How do I know?
You said so.

Rare Occasions

Lord, help me
To listen patiently
On those rare occasions
When my husband
Takes me in his arms
And tells me
How wonderful he is.

I'm Coming Home

Forgive me, Lord...
For pretending so much
And producing so little.
For shouting so boldly
And living so fearfully.
For condemning in my mate
The very faults I attempt to hide.
For beginning so often
And finishing so seldom.
For kicking like a stubborn colt
When life seems geared against me.
I'm so tired of it all, Lord.
Now at long last
With joyful anticipation
I'm coming home to my mate
And home to You.

Home To Stay

I love the story of the prodigal son
But so often, Lord
I wish there were another story
To ease my haunting conscience.
The prodigal son came home—to stay.
But I seem to be forever
Going and coming...
Going and coming...
The truth is—
I scarcely give You time in between
To fatten the calf!
Another thing, Lord
How many calves are there?
How many gold rings?

My one glad, glorious consolation is this:
Never once have You failed
To rush toward me with extended arms
When I finally came trudging home.
But I'm tired of it, Lord—
Just so tired of running.
When temptation nags at me again
When it comes in wild, rhythmic waves
Please remind me of the agony I suffer
The unendurable guilt, the torture
Every time I run from my Father!

Time

O God
I know I don't have to live
In a constant whirlwind
To prove I'm a capable homemaker
Or a committed wife.
I know, too
That You haven't chosen one wife—me—
To shortchange on time.
I have as much time as anybody else.
I know I am too often
Spinning like a top
Because I disregard my limitations.
I know my feverish flurry
Makes me depressed and irritable.
I know *all* these things, Lord
But I need Your grace
To do something about them.
Teach me what it really means
To be still and let you be God.
Remind me day by day
That dedicated weakness
Is far more precious to You
Than egocentric efficiency.
May I begin each morning
With a disciplined quiet time
To get Your perspective *all* the time.

What You
Ask Me To Do

Lord, the words of the Apostle Paul
Come weaving through my consciousness:
"I can do everything God asks me to do...."
I claim this victorious affirmation
For my own busy schedule today.
But first I need Your gentle reminder
That Your power is released
For what *You* ask me to do.

I confess, Lord
Too often my motives are mixed.
Too often my secret desire for approval
Pushes me into tasks and assignments
I should never accept.
Too often I burden myself with nonessentials
In a futile attempt to escape Your call
To quiet meditation and prayer.
Forgive me, Lord!
I am either monopolized by trifles
Or swept in by enormous "worthy causes."
Today I ask for guidance
To do lovingly, faithfully, joyfully
Only what You ask me to do
In the time You give me to do it.

Sorting Things Out

Lord, what's wrong with me today?
I don't like myself at all!
Maybe it's the weather
(Will it ever stop raining?)
Or maybe it's my unmanageable hair.
I'm in an awful rut.
I've just got to try a new hairstyle.
I wonder—
Could I be covering up a sense of guilt
About the two new dresses I bought
When I really didn't need them?

If I could just analyze it, Lord!
I have so much to thank You for
Yet here I am feeling jittery, dull
And totally unresponsive.
In a few minutes my husband will be home.
Don't let me take my brooding out on him.
When he walks through the door
Weary and hungry
Give me at least sufficient grace
To say a cheerful hello.
Then when he takes his shower
Let it be a l-o-n-g shower, Lord.
I need a little more time
To sort things out.

Creative Task

Lord, You are giving me
The stupendous task
Of helping my husband become
All You intend him to be.
It startles me, God.
It overwhelms me.
I am a partner in Your creation!
Help me to love him
With all the love of my being.
Keep refueling me, God
For too often I run low on love.
And, Lord
Help me never to use "I love you"
As a crutch or a cover-up
When I should first say, "I'm sorry."

The Dilemma

Lord, I think I'm due
For a good old-fashioned cry.
I can feel it coming on
But I'm in a dilemma.
How shall I handle it, Lord?
Shall I cry it out now
While I'm here by myself
Or shall I wait until
My husband comes home
And use his broad shoulder?
Maybe I'd better cry now
And get it out of my system.
Then when he sees my red, puffy eyes
I'll at least have the aftermath
of this calming comfort
And dinner won't be quite so late.

Marks of Distinction

Lord, I'm discovering
There are two distinct ways
To bolster my shivering ego:
I can adopt the downgrade method
And berate my family and friends
With sarcasm and cutting remarks.
Or I can seek Your wisdom
In developing my own God-given talents
With Your distinguishing marks
Of poise, purpose, and power.
Knowing You as I do, dear Lord
I know what You're after:
Marks of distinction!

They Gave Up

A month before they were married
Still felling shaky and hesitant
Regarding their decision
They finally said to each other
"Well, let's give it a try.
If it works, fine—
If it doesn't, we can give up."
So in the course of a year
They made their personal contribution
To the astronomical figure
Of rising divorce statistics.
They gave up.

Words

I saw her drooping shoulders
Her sad, misty eyes
As his bitter words of sarcasm
Blew across her animation
And choked the story
She longed so much to share....

Words!
O dear God
Words can be so devastating
So destructive.
They shock and numb
They sting and torment.
In three brief minutes
They can disfigure a soul.
They permeate the air
Like a suffocating poison.
Lord, Your own Word convicts us:
"So also the tongue is a small thing
But what enormous damage it can do."
Teach us to cope tactfully
Even in moments of disagreement.
Make us carefully selective
And lovingly protective
In the creative use of words.

Total Means Total

The tall, strapping high schooler
Lingered after class to talk.
With hostility covering his hurt
He said with clenched fist
"If God could part the Red Sea
Why in the world couldn't He
Make my parents love each other?"
The answer is—He could
If there were a total willingness
On the part of each mate to let Him.
But total means exactly that—total!

To Love Is To Obey

I couldn't escape You, Lord
You kept nudging me...prodding me...
With ceaseless persistency.
I heard Your still small voice—
Until I could no longer withstand
The emotional burden.
At last I gave in to You.
"Yes, Lord, I'll go
Though it means revamping
My carefully arranged schedule.
I'll go—today."

At the front desk
Of a large convalescent hospital
A buxom nurse looked through her files.
"Room 312," she told me briskly.
As I walked down the corridor
I smiled at a pajama-clad man
Sitting in a wheelchair.
He didn't smile back.
I wanted to run...to escape....

Room 312...
Quietly I stood by her narrow bed
And looked down at her closed eyes
Her thin, drawn lips.
Gently I roused her.
For one fleeting moment
Her wrinkled face glistened.

She was beautiful again!
I caught her faltering words:
"I wanted to see you
More than anyone else
In all this whole world."

With all the love of my aching heart
I reached out to her.
I promised to come back.
I left the hospital and wept.
Two days later she died.

O God
What if I had not gone!
Help me never to ignore the urgency
Of Your still small voice.
Remind me persistently
That to love is to obey.

Poignant Hurt

Laughing raucously
He said to his chagrined wife
"I wouldn't eat that
If I were you, Fatty!"
All eyes turned toward her
And when I saw her poignant hurt
I wasn't at all surprised
That she weighed two hundred pounds.
What else did she have?

Never Too Late

Her phone bill will be staggering!
We talked long distance for over an hour
But how do you quiet love?
Excitedly she said
"I'm so in love.
He's everything I've ever wanted.
And oh, my dear
He treats me like a queen!"
Weaving in words between her delight
I finally managed to ask
"When will you be married?"
"A week from today," she exuded
"On my seventy-eighth birthday!"

How beautiful, Lord...
With You it's never too late.

The Fact Is...

At a Palm Springs swimming pool
I watched an attractive mother
Lean over the pool's edge
And beckon to her young daughter—
A beautiful child
(probably five or six)
Blonde ringlets framing her pixie face.
"Please let me stay, Mother...please!"
The mother was calm but insistent.
"We must meet your father
And there is no guard on duty.
Now don't ask again, Jennifer."

With small hands on shapeless hips
She came up the steps
Slowly...reluctantly...
Finally a burst of explosive tears.
"You don't love me, Mother.
You really don't love me!"
With beautiful gentleness
The mother drew the tiny frame
Close to her loving heart.
She ran her fingers through wet curls.
"I know it feels that way, honey—
Of course, it feels that way."
Then she spoke directly to me:
"But isn't it good that our feelings
Don't always fit the facts?"

Yes, Lord, yes!
When I feel I can't possibly make it
When I feel helpless
Against the sudden adversities
Tearing and twisting my life
The fact is...You have a plan!
The fact is...You will make a way!
You will never let go of my hand!
My feelings don't fit the facts!

Pathetically
Immature

I'm frightened for them, Lord
They're so in love
Yet so pathetically immature.
When I cautiously asked
"Why not wait for marriage
Until you have some financial reserve?"
They answered defiantly
"Oh, no! We want to be married.
Besides, we love each other so much
The money will take care of itself."

Lord, they're so right.
The money will take care of itself!
It will take care to drag them down
And rouse their suspicion and anger.
It will take care to create
Friction, tension, and worry.
It will take care to postpone payments.
It will take care to necessitate new loans.
It will take care to fill their mailbox
With notes and letters from creditors.
It will take care to destroy teamwork
And create continual anxiety.

Lord, show them their mistake!
They have no outside financial help.
Teach them to face facts realistically.
I don't ask that You increase their wisdom—
Just give them outright, as a special gift
The very beginning of wisdom.
Surely Your good and beautiful plan
For their young lives
Includes freedom from bondage.
Lord, they aren't married yet.
Give them a fervent desire to seek your will!

New Lease on Life

"I'm tired of the whole thing!"
She screamed.
"I want out—clear out!
I'm tired of dirty diapers
And mounds of dishes
And smelly refrigerators
And outrageous bills
And the struggle to survive.
Do you hear me?
I'm just plain tired!
I'm tired of pretending
And erupting inside
And groping to find my way.
I want to find out who I am.
I want a new lease on life!"

O God
Right now give me Your love
And Your divine wisdom
To help her understand
That what she really needs
Is a lease on new Life!

Prayer Request

Lord, perhaps I'm worrying too much
About my devoted friend
Who is so deeply spiritual.
She never misses a church service
Morning or night—
Even though on occasions
Her husband has begged her
To spend a weekend with him.
Every week she attends three study groups
And whenever there is a women's retreat
She's the first to register.
She reads avidly, Lord
Always earmarking pages
To read aloud to her husband.
When she leaves the house
With her Bible and notebook
He settles down with his own problems.
There is never time to voice them.

Lord, her prayer requests
Invariably include her husband:
"Please pray for him.
Our interests are so divergent
And I long for him to change."
Of course, her friends are praying.
And I am praying, too.
But do You mind, Lord
If I pray mostly for my friend to change?

Lord,
I Just
Keep
Running
in Circles

When I Cannot Utter a Word

Because of a strange chemical imbalance
My husband has lost his ability to speak.
He can hear me
He can understand me
But despite his longing desire
He cannot verbally respond.
The doctor assures me
The puzzling malady will pass.
However, he is not sure how soon.
I sit by the hospital bed
To watch and wait—
To fervently pray.
I hold my husband's hand.
Gently, ever so gently
I tell him of my love.
Through the long, difficult hours
I continually reassure him.
He hears me, I know he hears me.
In his tired eyes I see his love.
But he cannot utter a word...
Not a single word.

O dear God
When my emotions are drained
When my heart is empty
When my hopes seem strewn on a dusty road
How well I remember
How gently *You* reassured *me*.
Even when I cannot utter a word...
Not a single word.

I Was Furious

This morning
A cantankerous neighbor said to me
"Not only do you drive as well
As your husband drives
But you can do it
On either side of the road!"
She laughed raucously as she said it
But I was just furious!
Not only do I drive a little better
Than my husband drives
But I *never* drive
On the wrong side of the road.
Lord, could we move?

Child, could you forgive?

I Can Settle for That

The word *rebellion* frightens me.
I always associate it with
Revolt...terrorism...riots...death...
With economic and social issues...
With the drug scene
That promotes life without purpose.
I associate it with tempestuous waves of change
That leap up like wild animals.
Like the disciples in the storm
I want to awaken You, Lord.
I wonder why You seem to be sleeping.

But, Lord, maybe I don't
Really know You very well.
Maybe I don't let God be God.
After all, *You* are not frightened.
You do not hold Your hands up in despair.
You never say,"You should have come yesterday,"
Nor do You say, "You're the wrong age and color."
You never say, "You're too timid, too slow."

You simply tell me to step out
Of my rocking boat.
You tell me to walk the waves with You.
You assure me You are not asleep.
You tell me to show genuine love
To a desperately needy world.

You insist it is far better
To walk over the billows than to go under them.
You tell me if I die in the attempt
At least I will die victoriously.
Then, facing me directly, You ask
"Can You settle for that?"
Lord, if You are with me
I can settle for that!

No Further

O God
So many things occur in my life
That are far, far beyond
My childlike comprehension.
My spirit is often bruised.
My thoughts are scattered.
I am left floundering and faltering.
There are shattering disappointments.
There are conflicts and doubts.
There are hours of emotional weariness.
And yet, the very thought
Of attempting to manage life without You
Brings more desolation
Than all other agonies packaged together.
I would rather endure the gigantic assaults
In Your presence, dear God
Than live a single day
Without Your hand of protection.
For Your words to the Enemy of my soul
Are as powerful for me
As they were for Job:
"This far you may go, but no further."

What Is Your Answer?

O God, I call to You
But there is no answer.
I search for You
But I cannot find You.
I cry, but You do not come.
I hurt, but You do not help.
I reach for Your hand
But there is only empty space.
O God
Does it matter to You about me?
If Your answer is no
Just whisper it.
If it is yes
Please shout it!

God, How Can I Describe You?

O God
How can I describe You?
To whom can You be compared?
Your Word says
No one in all the world
Can begin to fathom
The depth of Your understanding.
You sit above the circles of the earth.
You stretch out the heavens like a curtain.
You count the stars
To see that none of them have strayed.
You pick up the islands
As though they had no weight at all.
So why should I grapple
With a single lingering doubt
That You are powerful enough to hold me?

Urgent Request

Lord, You said in Your Word
I could talk to You
About anything—
Just *anything*, Lord.
So right at this precise moment
I have a very urgent request.
Will You please help me
Find my glasses soon enough
To remember why I needed them
In the first place?

The Deciding Factor

Years ago
When I was still in high school
My wise and experienced father
Suggested four pertinent questions
Regarding each pending decision:

Will the result harm me?
Will it strengthen and build me?
Will it benefit others?
Will it please God?

Lord, I am confident
That neither I nor others
Would be harmed
But rather strengthened
If I answer yes
To the pending issue.
But, God, how can I know assuredly
That *You* will be pleased?

My child
Let my ruling peace
Be the deciding factor.

My "Beautiful Thoughts"

The other night at the dinner table
When our guests were sharing
personal ideas and experiences
I watched carefully
For a break in the conversation
Which somehow never came.
I was especially eager
To share the "beautiful thoughts"
That had so inspired me
During my quiet time earlier that day.
At the end of the evening
After our guests had said good-night
I was pricked with slivers of guilt.
I wondered, Lord
What had been my greatest concern...
My unshared "beautiful thoughts"
Or the transforming power
Of Your Word itself?

Running in Circles

Lord
Why do I feel so uncertain?
I am always wondering
If I've made the right decision
Or said the right thing
Or planned the right guest menu
Or given the right advice.
I wonder if I've chosen the right dress
Or the right color of carpeting.
Often I ponder whether I should have
Taken on a certain responsibility.
When I make a phone call
I sometimes fear I will be misunderstood.
I wonder if I'm trying to do too much
Or if I should be doing more.
Sometimes I worry that I don't pray enough
Or read Your Word enough
Or witness enough.
Lord, I feel so utterly helpless.
What in the world is wrong with me?
Why am I always running in circles?

Troubled child
Nothing you could do
Would ever be "enough."
Just leave yourself alone
And delight in Me.

Desperation

O God
I am so sidetracked
So hard-pressed
From every direction.
I can't concentrate
I can't relax.
I feel like I'm going up
On a coming-down escalator.
There is grocery shopping to do
There are six phone calls to make
I must bake a birthday cake
And plan a party
And scrub the kitchen floor
And take my sick neighbor some soup
And pick up my husband's suit
And water the plants in the backyard
And clean the patio
And...O Lord, I'm simply desperate.
How can I handle it all
Without falling apart?

My frenzied child
I never ask of you
More than one thing
At a time.

My Heart Rages

O God, forgive me for saying it
But often my heart rages
Against the horrendous injustice
Of undeserved suffering.
The insidious ravages of war
The hunger-cries of starving children
The innocent victims of incurable diseases
The tragic accidents snuffing out life
In a moment of time...
Years of intense agony
Surgeries
Financial drain
Fears, tears, loneliness
Unbearable loss.
O God, do You hear me?
Often my heart rages
Against the injustice of it all.

My dear child
So does Mine.

I Just Keep
Running in Circles

Often, Lord
I am too frantically busy
Getting nowhere fast.
I run, I rush
I grope for breath.
I start two new projects
Before finishing the last three.
I read but part of a book.
I reach for the broom
Before finishing the dusting.
In the middle of making a grocery list
I stop to make a telephone call.
It goes on and on like that
And then it gets worse!
I am like a seamstress busily sewing
Without a spool of thread on her machine.
Quiet me. Settle me. Establish me.
I'm so weary of running in circles.

High Pedestal

Lord, forgive me
For the times
I put myself
On a pedestal so high
That my husband
Can't reach me.
So often it is
When he needs me most.

The End of the Rope

O dear God
I feel as though I am clinging
To a rough, swinging rope.
Beneath me there is only emptiness.
My hands are bruised and bleeding.
There is no possible way
For me to tie a knot
At the end of the rope
And hang on.
O God, please help me.

Frightened child
Just let go.
I'll catch you.

The Deliberate No

O God, teach me to say
The deliberate and releasing word *no*
Without a spiritual tug-of-war
Between variations of false guilt.
May I say it tactfully
Kindly and gently
But enable me to *say* it!
If on occasions I am forced
To confront an honest doubt
May I wait patiently
For Your clear guidance.
May this powerful truth
Penetrate the inner chambers of my being:
It is better to say a God-guided no
Than a self-guided yes.
Lord, remind me often
That a squirrel cage
Can be mighty confining.
So can a heart attack
And a hospital bed.

Live by the Moment

O Lord
I am staggered by the enormity
Of the countless tasks
Flung at me today.
I simply don't know
How to tackle them all.
What shall I do first, Lord?
How shall I make room
For the interruptions
That are bound to come?
What shall I leave undone
When interruptions take priority?
Your Word clearly states
That You will guide me
With Your counsel.
You have promised Your wisdom
When my lack is so great.
I dare not plunge into the day
Without seeking Your guidance.
Lord, will You help me?

Anxious child
Live today
By the moment
Not by the year.

Renewed Commitment

Forgive me, dear Lord
For too often
Letting the painful memories
Of my yesterdays
Crowd out the glad tomorrows
You graciously offer me.
I know I cannot rekindle
The charred embers
Of the past year.
I cannot erase the blunders
Made so impulsively
Nor can I regain the opportunities
That are forever lost.
I cannot retract the impetuous words
I wish I had not spoken
Or replace the shallow choices
I should not have made.
But I *can* open my wayward heart
To Your cleansing power.
With honest determination
I *can* renew my broken vows.
And I *can* begin to praise You
This very day
For the joy of beginning again.

Sullen Child

Today I identify with Job
When he said he was reduced
To egg white without salt.
A great loneliness consumes me
As I walk through faded leaves
That seem anxious to die.
The hills are brown and barren.
Not a single creative thought
Grips or challenges me.
Someone crossing the street calls
"Have a happy day!"
I'm tempted to answer
"No thanks."
O God, what is wrong with me?
Why do I feel so dull?
Why am I so listless?
Why do You seem so distant
When I feel so alone?

Sullen child
Why don't you
Fill your days
With praise?

Whistling in the Dark

Lord
Today as I contemplate
A third surgery
So quickly following the second
It all seems so dark.
To be very honest
Even the thought of
Whistling in the dark
Has very little appeal.
I've never whistled well.
I wonder—
Could my guardian angel
Whistle for me?
Sorry, Lord.
When it comes right down to it
I really don't need a whistler—
Not even an angel.
I just need You.

Unexplainable Mystery

Mysterious God
Today I am desolate
I am puzzled
I am heartsick
That I must wait so long
When You have promised so much.
At the same time
I am conscience-stricken
That I should feel such bitter rebellion.
Yet, to try to hide my emotions
Would only build up a pretense
That would eventually be exposed.
I suppose, O God
In the great perplexities
Of my unpredictable life
One of two things will always happen:
Either I will crowd You out
(Slowly but surely)
Or I will acknowledge Your sovereignty
In every area of my bewildered life.
To offer myself to You
Regardless of circumstances
May always bring unexplainable mystery.
But rejecting You totally
Brings the depth of despair.

One Request

God, I am determined to obey You
In what You have asked me to do
Even though at this moment I tremble
When I think of the possible consequences.
Nevertheless, should I choose
To ignore Your command
I fear even more the great personal loss
Disobedience eventually brings.
So, my Lord, I draw a deep breath
And deliberately step out
Into a seemingly reckless path.
I have but one request:
Please go before me and I will follow.

A Growing Marriage

Lord, we're still growing
In our marriage
And that's so good!
We're even doing better
When we criticize each other.
Like a gentle kitten
Courtesy is creeping in.
We feel the paws
Not the claws.

Submission

Dear God
When all my dreams shatter
When my plans go awry
When friendships cool
And neighbors annoy
Teach me to be submissive.
Enable me to say
As the Psalmist said
"O Lord, I adore you
As being in control of everything."

Your Child, God

O God
With deep contrition
I shamefully confess
My small concept of You
My puny faith
My limited comprehension.
Forgive me, O God
And enlarge my narrow vision.
Stimulate my trust
As I concentrate on Your greatness.
Give me even now
A true perspective
Of Your majestic power
To totally transform the child
On whom You have set Your love—
The child whose name is engraved
On the palm of Your hand
The child who claims You
As her Maker and Master.
Your child, God!
Me!

A Beautiful Plan

Lord, on this first day of January
I've thought of a beautiful plan
For challenging the winter doldrums:
Once a week, dear Lord
I'll make a phone call
To a friend, or to an acquaintance
I've never called before.
Once a week I'll write a note
To our mailman, or to our doctor
Or to the boy who mows our lawn—
A note of deep appreciation.
Once a week I'll extend
A coffee invitation to someone
Who has never been in our home.
Once a week I'll try a new recipe
Or clean a kitchen cupboard
Or a storage shelf in the garage.
Once a week I'll read a recommended book.
And once a week I'll surprise my husband
With a tiny love gift—something just for him.
Lord, I do hope You're pleased with my plan.
Now please help me to do it
At least the first week!

Excuses

O God
I've become a self-educated master
Of a thousand polished excuses.
Hoping to avoid Your penetrating gaze
I clutch them to me like valuable gems.
When I think I have myself thoroughly covered
I'm caught short with the realization
That You see right through me.
My flimsy excuses are never really hidden.
I find an excuse for all my failures
Wrong choices
Late appointments
Wasted time.
I excuse my foolish blunders, my laziness
My broken resolves, my unreached goals.
I need Your help, Lord!
To hide from You is as foolish
As the Grand Canyon
Attempting to hide from the sky.
O God, my only hope
Lies in Your invincible power
To make me what I am not yet
But what you know I can become.
Strengthen my will, Lord.
Make me firm, steadfast, consistent.
Control my impulses, my emotions.
May I keep pursuing and never quit.

Boundless Love

Lord, yesterday at the sunny beach
I traced crooked lines in the sand
With a small, damp twig.
The wet spray blew against my face
And a thousand thoughts
Went tumbling into the frolicking waves.
When I talked to You I heard You say
"My boundless love surrounds you."

Today I am at home again
Fixing meals, washing dishes
Talking on the phone, answering mail—
All the ordinary things, Lord.
When I talk to You I hear You say
"My boundless love surrounds you."
And dear God, suddenly I know
It is as true in my home today
As it was yesterday at the sunny beach!

I Plead with You

Lord of my longing heart
I plead with You
To help me want *You*
More than I want *this*.
The unquenchable desire within
Is so overpowering, so consuming
At times I think
I can no longer endure it.
I think I would rather die
Than live without
That which so completely absorbs me.
And yet, dear God
There is the unwavering conviction
That what I want
Is not what You want for me.
There is the deep certainty
That the day would come
When my personal choice
Would close every future open door.
Lord, I cannot handle this alone.
I am not strong enough
Nor am I willing enough.
You alone can change my heart's desire.
You alone can make all things new.
O dear Lord, please help me
To want *You* more than I want *this*.

As You Have
Forgiven Me

Lord, all week long
I have struggled painfully
With the agony of unforgiveness.
In clinging to my hidden resentment
My spirit has been consumed.
Channels of creativity have been clogged.
I have been brittle, evasive, unyielding.
I've winced and wallowed in self-pity.
My health has been affected.
To pray has been a heavy burden.
I am starkly aware that I cannot afford
The luxury of an unforgiving heart
Unless I need no forgiveness from You.
There is no more room in my heart
For the twisting torment of this past week.
I am willing to drop the offense.
Now, dear Lord, please cleanse me.
Release me, purify me
And empower me to forgive
As freely as You have forgiven me.

The Conclusion

Lord, Lord
I am not as brave
As You seem to think
Nor as strong
Nor as capable of standing firm
In the midst of affliction.
Lord, there is not a drop
Of emotional response in me.
No awareness of Your love
No comfort or joy in Your promises.
I have no deep conviction
That You are real.
There is no daylight in my heart
Nor even candlelight.
Nevertheless, with sheer determination
And perhaps a bit of spiritual grit
I have opted to throw my weight
On Your word *without*
Rather than my feelings *within*.
I don't know exactly when it happened
But I have reached the conclusion
That I would rather walk with You
In the dark of night
Than walk without You
In the light.

Telltale Signs

I begin to see
All these little telltale signs
That remind me starkly
I'm no longer thirty years old—
Or even forty or fifty years old.
Last Christmas was a good example.
I prided myself on shopping early
But when it was time to wrap the gifts
I couldn't remember where I had hid them.
Please, dear Lord
Keep me smiling!
I have a strange feeling
It gets worse rather than better.

So Ashamed

I whimpered through my work this morning
As though I were the only one
In the entire world
With an ache or pain.
Late this afternoon my sister called
To tell me she must once again
Face the dreaded trauma of chemotherapy.
Just a year ago her husband died.
As we talked she said
"I have been listening to tapes
Of his wonderful sermons
And I am so comforted...
So comforted..."
Lord, I remember my morning whimper
And I am so ashamed...
So ashamed.

A Watered Garden

O dear God
I don't want to be
A plastic flower
Without life
Without fragrance
Without growth.
I want to be real!
Transplant me if You must.
Root me, cultivate me
Water me, weed me.
Send the rain
Send the sun
Until I am like a watered garden
delighting the heart of my God!

Your Way, Lord

Lord, in no way do I claim the right
To "program" my own life.
Nor do I want to feed my own
Unmanageable impulses.
I am not asking today
For time to do this or that.
I simply ask for renewed energy
To do joyfully and willingly
Whatever You want me to do
In the time You give me to do it.

Settled Decision

God, it is my settled decision
Not to choose less
When You have chosen more for me.
Not to choose the worst
When You have chosen the best.
Not to stoop to defeat
When You have provided victory.
Not to let my emptiness
Close the door to Your fullness.

Tribute

Lord, how can I adequately thank You
For a husband whose commitment
Remains solid and steadfast
Through forty-three years of marriage?
How can I thank You for his reassuring smile?
His sound judgments?
His wise counsel?
Through the cumulative years
He has so often fortified my faith.
With gentle understanding
He has reestablished my wavering values.
When the fogs of life
Have been unusually dense
He has stood faithfully by my side.
When I've been caught in the tangles
Of anxiety and stress
He has helped me put things together again.
He has brought gigantic joy into my life.
And always, Lord
He is my reason for wanting to hurry home.

Take Joy

I see them on skateboards
As they skate by our yellow house.
I see baseballs and bats
And transistor radios
Strapped securely to shoulders.
I see bright sweatshirts
And worn shoes, and crazy hats.
I see a little guy with a red wagon
Who stoops to examine a parade of ants.
Then, with a small twig
He casually pushes the ants aside.
His faithful mongrel watches and waits.
I hear squeals of laughter
And hilarious comments.

It's Saturday! No school!
A day of freedom, a day for fun.
Freedom to ride, to run, to hike.
Freedom to explore new trails
To breathe the fragrance of spring.
Freedom to drink in the warmth of the sun.
I'm happy...happy for *their* happiness.
I remember similar Saturdays of long ago
And the exhilarating sense of freedom.

But suddenly I remember, too
How transitory happiness is.
So quickly it can be brushed aside
By corroding circumstances.

I long to call, to shout:
"Hey, kids, listen!
Take a minute and listen.
Open your young hearts to *joy*...
The joy that comes from God alone.
It's so different from happiness.
It's real, it's permanent.
Nothing can destroy it:
Neither tears nor pain nor tragedy.
Whatever else you may lose
In the shuffle of life
Joy you may keep forever.
Hey, kids, listen!
Take God's word for it.
It's His personal gift.
His Son made it possible.
You'll never regret it.
I know! I know!
Take joy!"

Prayer for a Husband

Lord, on this first day of the new year
I pray for my husband—
Your dearest love-gift to me,
May he enjoy vibrant health
And a sense of deep satisfaction
In the work You've chosen for him.
Enlarge his vision.
Give him full knowledge of Your will.
Keep him calm and objective
In every difficult situation.
Fulfill his high expectations, Lord.
Encourage and uphold him.
Above all, give him, I pray
A very personal relationship with You.
I claim for him Your promise to Abraham:
"I will bless you
And you shall be a blessing."
Lord, what more could I ask
For the husband who is more than life to me?

Lessons in Patience

Dear Lord
After forty-three years of marriage
I think perhaps I've learned
A few practical lessons in patience.
For example, it isn't always easy
To laugh at my own jokes.
Especially when we have dinner guests
And my husband tells *my* jokes.

Empower Her Today

Lord, despite what she tells me
Of her unquenchable love
For the husband of the other woman
She is cheating herself so terribly.
She is putting a million-dollar investment
Into a ten-cent ride.
She is like a child
Who purchases a dime-store diamond
Giddily pretending it's the real thing.

How will she explain your unchanging values
To her own lovely daughter
Who will soon be twelve?
How will she guide her
In the swift approaching years
When *she* must work through temptation?
How will she protect her
Against the fiery emotions
That entangle so rapidly?

Purity is not a harsh, hissing word.
Purity is Your word, Lord.
O God, burn within my confused friend
The inescapable truth
That "free" love is never free...
That physical intimacy will disintegrate
Unless it serves Your plan and purpose...
That she cannot break Your commands
Without breaking something immeasurably sacred
Within her own God-planned life.

Lord, she is Your child.
A hundred times she has said
"If only I knew the right way."
Deep in her homesick heart she does know.
Empower her to walk it—*today.*

Confession

O God
You are the Creator
Of light and darkness
Sun and rain
Summer and winter
Streams and desert
Great and small.
You give laughter and tears
Victory and trials.
And yet, I frankly confess
I find it painfully difficult
To praise You equally
For laughter *and* tears.

Salt and Stardust

Lord, through the years
We are learning
That marriage is a combination
Of salt and stardust—
Salt for hamburgers
And stardust for poetry.
Undoubtedly we could survive
A little longer on hamburgers
Than we could on poetry.
But why should we settle for one
When we know You want us to have both?

Frustrated Desires

All day long, dear Lord
Her haunting words
Have swept through my aching heart.
"Frustrated desires..."
Together we stood at the card rack
Looking at birthday cards.
Wanting to be friendly
I said nonchalantly
"It's difficult to choose
When they're all so beautiful."
She looked toward me pensively.
"My husband died three months ago.
We always gave each other
Beautiful cards.
Today is his birthday.
I wish I could give him
The whole rack."
Pushing back the tears
She said half-apologetically
"I'm sorry, I didn't mean
To trouble you
With my frustrated desires."

I cannot comfort her, Lord.
I don't even know her name.
She left the store so quickly.
But not for a single moment
Is she lost to You.
Wherever she is right now
Hold her close to Your loving heart.
Comfort her, quiet her, dear God
And transform her frustrated desires
Into happy, heart-shaped memories
Until she is able to say
With trust and confidence
"Nothing can separate me
From the love of God."

A New Suit

Lord, I want to talk to You
About a very personal matter.
Perhaps You will smile—
But why is it so difficult
To persuade my husband
To shop for a new suit?
He *needs* a new suit.
He can *afford* a new suit.
I'll gladly shop with him
When he can be persuaded to go.
It's not that he flatly refuses—
He just keeps putting it off.
"Maybe next week," he said this morning.
It's the twinkle in his eye
That finally dissolves my exasperation.
A friend told me to be grateful.
"After all," she said
"When a husband has but one suit
He can always find his car keys."
Frankly, I hadn't thought of that.
So when the day finally comes
That we take the great plunge
We'll visit the locksmith, too.
Lord, Your Word specifically says
You changed the mind of a king.
So please hear my request
And change my husband's mind, too.

Off-Track Life

God, though she is only in college
Already she is steeped in fear
And shattered with guilt.
With aching agony
She longs for inner peace.
I find it difficult
To know how to help her
In her bewilderment
And self-condemnation.
Nevertheless, I have promised
To stand by her side
Through the pitch-black tunnel
Of her off-track life.
But in the darkness, dear God
May I gently remind her
That I cannot give her light.
You alone can do that.

The Search

There is scarcely a day
That she does not argue with someone.
If it is not with her husband
It is with her mother
Or with her husband's mother.
Often she argues with her children.
Again and again she argues with friends.
When she grocery shops
She argues over prices and brands.
Sometimes I think her tirades
Are sort of a challenge
To see how long she'll be withstood.
But somehow in her arguments
I hear overtones of deep yearnings.
She seems to be seeking a way
Out of her personal dungeon.
Yet she is afraid of the light.
I wonder, dear God...
Is her greatest battle with herself?
Or is her most crucial argument with You?
God, I long for her to experience
Your liberating power
But when she begins to argue
We come to a standstill.
I am at a loss to know how to help her.

Dear child
Share your victories
But confess your defeats.
Share the light
But confess that there are shadows.
When she knows she is not alone
Her desperation will subside
And her search for Me will begin.

The Greatest Need

Lord, how can I help this woman
Who is coming to have tea with me today?
She wants to discuss her personal problems
But I find it difficult to talk to her.
Trying to get a word in edgewise
Is like trying to thread a sewing machine
With the motor running.
She says she simply has no time
To get everything done.
She bemoans the fact
That she's always running in circles.
But when I try to make suggestions
About managing her time
She stands up vigorously in her own defense
And falls down miserably on her priorities.
I'm sorry, Lord
But I really feel she does me more harm
Than I do her good.

Dear child
Just listen to her.
She needs that most.

The Gift

Lord
The shopping is finished
The gifts, beautifully wrapped
Are placed with gentleness
Under our smiling tree.
We chose carefully, Lord
Just the right gifts
For those who are so dear to us.

Today I am suddenly aware
That long years ago
In the fullness of time
You sent the Gift of Your Son
Because we are so dear to You!
O God, thank You!

Grandfather

He never headed a great corporation.
He was not a college president
Or an author or a financier.
His academic education concluded
In a shabby red schoolhouse
With a potbellied stove.
Every Sunday morning, rain or shine
He sat in the same pew
Of a tall-steepled country church.
If anyone had asked him to repeat
The main points of a sermon
He could not have done it
Had his life depended on it.
At the end of the service
He cautiously felt his way
Down the narrow aisle
To shake an outstretched hand
Or to rumple a tousled head.
When someone suggested he teach a class
He declined with a hearty laugh:
"I don't know too much theology—
Most of my learnin' is Doxology!"
But how he extolled You, dear God.
What honor he brought to Your name!
His grandson said it beautifully:
"He was a walking demonstration
Of a man who lived for God."

The Gain
Is All Theirs

O dear God
How they must love heaven—
My precious parents
Who made earth so rich
While they were here.
This very day
They laugh with fullness of joy
Serve with fullness of commitment
And praise with fullness of exaltation.

Never again need they
Ponder or analyze.
Never again need they
Ask Your forgiveness.
Never again need they sense
The slightest disappointment
Or question the wisdom
Of their decisions.
Singing without sorrow
Gladness without gloom
Delight without despair!
O dear God
The pain is on our side
The gain is all theirs.

Halloween Night

Halloween night...
Winds tingling...air cool and crisp
Goodies stacked near the door
Porch light blazing...
Squeals of laughter
Ghosts, clowns, Mickey Mouse
Indians, ballet dancers...
Seven-fifteen...eight-thirty
A few late stragglers
Finally a chance to eat our dinner.

Then a sort of shuffling sound
The doorbell again.
He stood there alone
A gruesome mask covering his face
So small, so young.
I knelt down to face him directly.
With mock seriousness, I said
"You really scare me!
I'd better close the door—quick!"
He lifted the corner of his mask.
"Do you want to see how I *really* look?"
I saw twinkly brown eyes
A freckled nose
A please-love-me grin.
We hugged each other—hard.

O God
In this crowded world of many masks
Please forgive my lack of compassion.
Remove my own pretenses
Until I see *persons*
Created in Your image
For Your divine purpose.
Above all, dear God
Make me a channel of Your *unmasked* love.

Stark Reality

He is forty-two years old.
All his erratic life
He has been making feeble excuses
For his wasted years
His lack of discipline
His refusal to accept responsibility.
Yesterday he said
With exaggerated gestures
"Remember the old proverb
'Eat, drink, and be merry
For tomorrow we die'?"

But, Lord
The stark reality is this:
In all probability
Tomorrow he will *not* die.
Tomorrow...and tomorrow
He will look back
And remember.

Gift Exchange

She is lonely
So at loose ends with herself
A sorry picture of dejection.
I had hoped to encourage her when I said
"To some God gives the gift of marriage
To others the gift of *not* being married."
She pushed back a strand of blonde hair
And asked ruefully
"Have you ever been given a gift
That you wanted to exchange?"
I didn't quite know how to answer her.
Lord, what should I have said?

The Family of God

In the family of God
We need not pretend to be
What we know we are not.
In the family of God
Our acceptance is not based
Upon how superbly we perform.
Our material possessions
Or lack of them
Are of little consequence.
Our personal failures
Do not shatter our relationships.
In the family of God
We are free to express
Our longing desires
Our loneliness, our fears
Our deep-seated frustrations.
In the family of God
We can freely acknowledge our needs
And expect the loving response
Of family members.
In the family of God
There is forgiveness
There is faith, there is hope
There is joy, there is love.
At least, dear God
This is your desire
For the family You dearly love.

Future Mates

Right now, dear Lord
Somewhere in this giant world
There is a young boy
For whom You have
A unique and special plan.
He may be pulling a wagon
Or fishing by a stream
Or stuffing cookies into his pocket.
His eyes are blue or gray or brown
His hair—is it light or dark?
It doesn't really matter.
It only matters that You hold him close
As he learns to walk with You.
As he grows to be Your man
Give him wisdom from above.
Give him singleness of mind
And purity of heart.
May he set worthy goals
And dream big dreams.
Wherever he is, Lord
Keep him strong and safe
Until in Your own good time
In Your own incredible way
You bring them together
To love, honor, and cherish—
The precious newborn daughter
Who lives next door to us
And the boy who is known to You.

A Song of Praise

O God
Thank You for the sheer pleasure
Of waking up to a newborn day.
There is no possible way to know
What each day will bring...
Some days are warm and sunny.
Others are damp and overcast.
Often I awake to the sound of rain
Falling steadily on our roof.
There are days when a gentle wind
Hugs our sleepy house.
Some days I feel the chill
Of an early frost.
Other days the mountains
Are freshly blanketed with clean snow.
But just to put my feet on the floor
To stretch, to yawn, to breathe deeply
To pull back the drapes
And greet the dawn with a song—
What a challenge, what a gift!
Again today, dear Lord
I lift my joyful heart in praise
For Your marvelous treasure called *day*.

For Better, for Worse

Lord, over forty years ago
We made a solemn promise:
"For better or for worse."
Today we are stumbling through "worse."
Though our emotions are a bewildered mixture
Of agony and love, please quiet us, Lord
Free us from the desire to retaliate.
Above all, help us both to remember
We are as bound to our promise today
As we were yesterday
When we basked in the sunlight of "better."
Even now, dear Lord
Help us to make it better again
By not putting off what we both know
We must eventually do
If healing is to take place.
The simple but beautiful word is forgiveness.

Crucial Decision

Lord, today I must make
A very crucial decision.
The decision will ultimately
Affect every area of my life—
Not only now, but in the years to come.
In my deepest heart I am convinced
That nothing is ever truly settled
Until it is settled right.
And nothing is ever settled right
Until it is settled with You.
God, You know my personal limitations
And my desperate need for Your help.
Please superimpose Your thoughts on my mind
And grant me the peaceful assurance
That I am following Your guidance.
I am so aware that the decision I make today
Will be inherited by those I love—tomorrow.

At Long Last

O Lord
At long last
I have placed in Your hands
The strong and aching desire
Which for so many months
Completely absorbed me.
Now to my surprise and delight
I have made the joyful discovery
That all my tenacious resistance
Was far more painful, more agonizing
Than a total letting go
In obedience to Your command.

My child
So it will always be.

After All,
There Is God

She came for her piano lesson
With a big chunk of news for me.
She was going to have tonsil surgery.
Naturally we had to talk about it.
I asked, "Are you scared, Susie?"
Only a moment's pause.
"Not very. Just a tiny bit scared."
"You're very brave, Susie.
I'd probably be very frightened."
Her flashing smile put the sun to shame.
"No, you wouldn't. After all, there *is* God."

O God, Susie is right!
Whatever the emergencies, the anxieties
The twistings and turnings
The crushing sorrows
There is God.
To trust You in the darkest night
Simply because of who You are
Because You are good
Because You are in control—
This is the secret of serenity.
God, make it *real* in my life
Not just something I read in a book.
May I give You the joy
Of total confidence in You.

Songs of Celebration

With overflowing gratitude
The Psalmist said
"We will write songs
To celebrate Your mighty acts!"
Lord, on the keyboard
Of my grateful heart
I too have composed many songs
To celebrate Your unequalled greatness
Your faithfulness
Your splendor and majesty.
Lord, the most triumphant song of all
Exalts Your measureless love.
With joy and adoration
I sing it again and again.
As long as I live, O God
I shall continue to sing
My songs of exuberant praise!

My Heart's Desire

O dear God
What joy, what tremendous exaltation
King David must have experienced
When he said to You triumphantly
"How the king rejoices
In Your strength, O Lord!
For You have given him his heart's desire—
Everything he asked You for!"
Now, dear God
Please hear my request as You heard David's.
With my whole heart
I want *from* You
Everything You want *for* me.
Then I too shall be able to say
"You have given me my heart's desire—
Everything I asked You for!"

I Wait for You

O God
I have waited so long
Under dark clouds of trial and testing
And yet Your promise is clear and precise:
"Blessed are all those that wait for Him."
Though I see no glimmer of hope
Though my tears come unbidden
I am still waiting
For the clouds of trial
To break into refreshing showers of blessing.
Because You have promised, dear Lord
Surely my waiting cannot be in vain.
I wait for You...I wait for You...I wait.

The Glory of God

Dear God
Too often my spoken words
Are sadly inconsistent
With my unspoken thoughts.
Too often my prayers for purity
Are inconsistent with my deliberate wrongs.
Too often my expressed resolves
Are inconsistent with my hidden faults.

The Psalmist said so magnificently
"The heavens are telling the glory of God...
Without a sound or word
Their message reaches out
To all the world."
God of all creation, recreate me.
Restore my wayward heart.
Blot out all sham and shame.
Day and night
Without a sound or word
May the purity of my life
Display the glory of God.
Wherever You place me
May the message reach out
To all the world.

All Night Long

Lord, thank You!
All night long I stayed awake with You.
We shared the hours together
From nine o'clock until early dawn.
I wasn't disturbed or anxious.
I just felt wonderfully close
To Your loving heart.
My husband slept.
My family slept.
As far as I know, my neighbors slept.
But You and I were awake, dear Lord.
I told You my intimate longings
My deepest desires.
Even my gross failures, Lord—
The ones I was so reluctant to confess.
And You shared shining secrets with me.
Secrets that will, I trust
Make me a more obedient child.
Your Word says so clearly
You neither slumber nor sleep.
I wonder...did You enjoy my company
As much as I enjoyed Yours?
Oh, Lord, I hope so!
For me it was a night I'll never forget.

The Birds Are Back

This morning at the breakfast table
A full flock of birds
Descended on our front lawn
Singing their hearts out!
In his prayer my husband said
"Lord, how we thank You
That the birds are back!"
At that moment I thought of the trauma
Of the mysterious past year.
Heartache, disappointment, pain
Despair, death, change.
Then I remembered Paul's wonderful words:
"Nevertheless afterward..."
With a glad heart I too rejoice
That the birds are back.
On this beautiful spring morning
I am singing with them.

For So Long

For so long, dear Lord
I have tried to fit You
Into my personal plans.
I've tried to crowd You in, somehow
Between my own chosen priorities.
Now at long last
I ask You to fit *me* into *Your* plans.
Mold me, teach me, use me
In whatever way will honor You.
O dear Lord
Give Yourself a magnificent reputation
In my God-planned life.

Hold Me Close

A little while ago
I said to my husband
"You're very quiet tonight—
You've spoken only a few words.
Is everything all right?"
"Everything is fine," he said.
"I really don't think
We need a lot of words.
I just want to hold you close."

Lord, sometimes
When You seem so silent
Is it that way with You?
Do You just want to hold me close?
If so, forgive me
For flinging my whys
And begging for explanations.
Forgive me for complaining about delays.
Help me just to quietly rest
In the shelter of Your arms
While You hold me close.

Wherever I Look

Lord, wherever I look I see spring!
Pansies and yellow daffodils
Border the green lawns
All over our neighborhood.
The graceful trees are branching
In every direction.
Shining leaves are eagerly
Getting acquainted with each other.
The password this morning is Joy.
Joy laughing and singing
And chasing sunbeams all over the hills.
To me it seems to have happened overnight.
Yet I know you have been quietly preparing it
For many long months.
Lord, help me to wait patiently
For "spring" in my life
When the winter months seem endlessly long.

Indescribable Joy

O God, thank You!
Today I learned
With indescribable joy
That one solid hour
Of drastic obedience
To Your command
Is a thousand times
More rewarding
Than months of frantic shouting
"Tomorrow, Lord
Tomorrow...tomorrow."

A Valuable Lesson

Thank You, Lord
For teaching us a valuable lesson
In our search for the pot of gold
At the end of the rainbow.
We've learned to pick up
A little silver here and there
Along the rugged way.
It's the silver that helps us
Pay our bills on time each month.

Lord, It
Keeps
Happening
...And
Happening

Not Sure Yet

In our challenging discussion
I started to tell my college friend
That though I didn't understand electricity
I certainly accepted it.
With an impatient gesture he interrupted me.
"I don't want to hear about electricity.
I just want God."
"How much do you want him?" I asked.
Nervous silence. Then finally a reply:
"I'm really not sure yet."

Lord, I don't know how long
My seeker-for-God friend
Will continue his flimsy excuses
Or linger in a state of noncommitment
But when he is sure enough to really seek You
He will surely find You.
This is Your personal promise.

All

O God
Thank You, thank You
For Your reiterated ALL...

You have promised:
    ALL my needs shall be supplied.
    ALL grace shall abound toward me.
    ALL the promises are mine.
    ALL things I ask I shall receive.
    ALL sufficiency for ALL things.
    You are with me always
    ALL the days.
    And today!

The Exception

Lord, too often I demand
From my family and friends
More love
More affirmation
More acceptance
Than they are capable of giving.
Today, dear God
I ask You to burn this truth
Into the depth of my inner being:
Nobody in all the world
Can ever love me
As much as I need to be loved—
Except You!

Happy Birthday

Today is my birthday, Lord
And birthdays always excite me.
I am so like a child
Breathlessly anticipating the surprises
Of a fresh, untarnished year.
As I reach out
Toward whatever moments or days
You entrust to me
Will there be drastic changes?
Will I be different?

My child
You are now
And always will be
Whatever you are willing
To let my love
Make of you.
Happy birthday!

Turnabout

God, for so long
I thought that by praying
I could change Your mind.
Often I prayed
Fervently, pleadingly
Until I felt
Emotionally pulverized.
Then I gradually began to grasp
That the purpose of prayer
Is to find *Your* mind
And let You change mine.
Little by little
The turnabout is renewing me.
Slowly I begin to feel
A settling quietness.
I wait while You woo me
To Your will, dear Lord.
I wait until my thoughts
Harmonize with Yours.
For in my deepest heart
Despite my guarded resistance
I somehow sense
That what You want for me
Is stupendously more
than anything I could
Dream or wish or want
For myself.

Commonplace Days

Lord of my commonplace days
Forgive me for foolishly waiting
For "divine inspiration"
Before moving in on the tasks
Personally assigned to me.
Hopefully I am learning
To face with greater determination
The day-by-day drudgery
The trite, mundane tasks
The pushing-pulling glamourless duties.
Lord, even I think
I'm getting no place
Keep me pushing on and on
With purpose and direction.
Grab my heart and quiet me
When I begin to whine and whimper.
Despite the daily drain
I think I see it more clearly now:
It is only when I begin to *do*
That You begin to *bless.*

Unnecessary

How patiently You wait, dear God
Until having battered myself
Against the impregnable wall
Of my own selfishness and rebellion
I turn at last
Broken and bruised
Into Your wide-open arms.
It is then that I learn
That all my struggling, my panic
My foolish pretenses were unnecessary—
Had I simply fallen trustingly
Into Your waiting arms
At the very beginning.

Good Morning, Lord!

Good morning, Lord!
At the fresh, fragrant beginning
Of this new-born day
I give You my will
To blend with Yours.
I give You, in fact
My total self.
As I yield to Your instructions
I am joyfully confident
That You will take care of the obstructions.

How To Entertain

Lord, I'm so glad
We don't have to be creative geniuses
Or serve elegant gourmet meals
To make our guests feel warm and wanted.
We need rather to expose them to love
And introduce them to laughter.
We need to listen
And never drown them out.
Above all, we need to remember
That there is no substitute—
None whatever—
For concentrated sharing
And genuine caring.

Slow Growth

In my fretful impatience
I am so often inclined to ask
"Why can't she change?"
"Why is he always so slow?"
"Will they ever learn from past mistakes?"
And then You begin to impress me
With my own slow progress upward.
I see Your stretched-out patience.
I remember how long You've waited for me.
And I grieve that my attitude
Is so often intolerant.
O God, keep fresh the imprint
Of my own need to grow
And make me more flexible
More understanding
And always more loving.

I Praise You

I praise You, my Lord!
I praise You for all things:
For this very moment
For future days
For the past
Often so reckless
On my part
So filled with
Foolish fantasies.
But so gracious
On Your part
So loving
And so totally forgiving.
I praise You!

The You Means Me

O my Father, my Father!
At this crisis time of my life
When I feel trampled and battered
I know it is imperative
For me to remember
That the nature of my problem
Is not the significant thing.
The significant thing
Is the nature of You
My refuge. My rock.
My high tower.
There is no situation
Anytime, or anywhere
Of which I cannot confidently say
"For this I have Him."
But I am so quick to forget
And so prone to neglect.
Lord, may I get it settled
Once and for all
That when You say
"My peace I give unto you"
the *you* means *me!*

Suddenly or Finally

Right now, dear God
In my bewildering day of turmoil
I call upon You
With unashamed boldness.
I come to You directly
Before seeking out family or friends.
You have promised to extricate me
According to Your infallible Word.
I offer You now my sacrifice of praise
For I know my deliverance will come.
"He is faithful that promised."
And, dear Lord, when You do deliver me
Whether it be suddenly or finally
I pledge my continual gratitude.
In fact, You'll never hear the end of it!

The Hardest Thing

O God
In these crisis days
Of piercing pain
And emotional fatigue
Do a brand new thing in me.
Give me water in the wilderness
And streams in my desert.
You have promised to be my God
Through all my lifetime.
Surely You will keep Your word!

As You promised
Give me rest from my sorrow
And from my fear
And from the bondage
That binds me.
One thing more, dear Lord:
Enable me to praise You
When to praise
Is the hardest thing of all.

Always Thinking

Thinking, always thinking...

Again today, dear Lord
I think of my friend
And the miserable quarrel
That shattered our friendship
After years of beautiful closeness....

I think of the soloist
I refuse to acknowledge
On a worshipful Sunday morning
Because of envy and pride...

I think of the young mother
Down the street
Deserted and divorced
Picking up bits and pieces....

The wrinkled old woman
Languishing in a rest home
Who for many faithful years
Taught me from God's Word....

Thinking, always thinking....

Lord, if suddenly You said
"This is your last week
On the planet called Earth"
How quickly, how spontaneously
My thoughts would convert to action.
How eagerly I would do
In seven short days
What You've persistently pressed upon me
For the past several months.
Lord, is it too late?

"And they immediately...followed him"

(Matthew 4:20)

Painfully New

O God
This sudden catastrophe
Is tearing my heart.
How can I endure it?
Why are You permitting it?
I know I am not alone.
All over the world
Your children are asking Why.
It's an old, old question—
As old as Job.
But today for me
It is painfully new.

I Trust

O God, thank You
That Your promises are valid
As long as the world lasts.
They do not suddenly dissolve
When my faith is feeble
And my courage fails.
When You have given a promise
You will perform it—
Sight or no sight
Feeling or no feeling.

You may take me
Through the darkest night
The deepest waters.
The very worst may happen
But out of it
You will bring the very best
For Your Word remains secure.

Lord, keep me faithful in my trust.
When I can articulate no other prayer
May my waiting heart
Continually avow:
I trust!
I trust!

Help Me To Listen

Dear Lord
Help me to *listen* to my husband
Without misinterpreting—
Without interrupting.
Don't let me color his words
With my own preconceived ideas.
Keep me from barging in
With "that reminds me..."
And, Lord, may I never use ridicule
As a symbol of superiority.

I Sing in the Rain

One cold, misty day
When I was nine years old
I walked hand-in-hand
Through a wooded forest
With my strong, gentle father.
"Listen to the stillness," he whispered.
"Stillness makes beautiful music."
Suddenly he pointed to a tiny bird
Perched on a limb of a bending tree.
"The bird doesn't know we're here
But he's singing his heart out."
Then smiling down at me he asked
"Could you sing in the rain
If nobody heard you but God?"

Lord, though many years have passed
Since I walked with my father
I have never forgotten his question.
Today I am alone—
Yet not alone, for YOU are here.
Though my heart is grief-drenched
I know You are worthy of praise.
Help me, please help me
To sing my feeble song in the rain
Though nobody hears but You.

Sane Estimate

Lord, help me to face with honesty
And genuine appreciation
The talents and abilities
You have given
As special gifts to me.
Give me a sane estimate of myself.
Neither exaggerated nor mud-crawling.
Just *sane*, as Your Word admonishes.
May I be joyfully satisfied
With Your unique plan for me.
When at times I'd secretly love to ride
On a colorful float
Beautifully adorned
Waving to cheering crowds
Smile at me, Lord.
With a twinkle in Your eye
Remind me again
That somebody has to build the float.

Memories

Dear God
How I thank You
For thousands of beautiful memories
That have become a growing history
Of Your supreme goodness in my life.
Thank You for misty memories
Flaming memories, trailing memories.
Thank You for throbbing memories
Quiet, gentle memories
Pink-tinted memories
That live on and on
To gladden somber days.
Thank You for memories that have rooted me
Stabilized me, sensitized me
And toughened the inner fiber of my being.
In Your honor, dear God
I erect my *Monument of Memories.*
For Your glory...You who are
My "living bright reality."

My Husband at Work

Lord
As my husband goes to his office today
I send him off with a hug and a prayer.
Thank You for the security I feel
In knowing You'll be with him all the way.
Protect him, dear God
As he maneuvers through heavy traffic.
Keep him relaxed as he changes lanes
And waits for signal lights.
Fill him with anticipation
Despite the annoyance he often feels
As he grapples with office personnel.
Should irritating problems remain unsolved
Please, Lord, lift him above them.
Make him resolute against discouragement.
May he *trust* Your guidance
Even though he may not *feel* it.
Whatever his achievements
Whatever his defeats
Bring him home at the end of the day
With the quiet assurance
That Your promises are positive
Your power exceeds all pressure
And our home is his fortress.

Explanation

Just this week
I read a newspaper account
Of a thirteen-year-old boy
Who saved his brother's life
By driving him to a hospital
In his father's car.
Never having driven before
His explanation was simple:
"I just did what I saw my father do."

O dear God
Please empower me to bring life
To a sick, wounded world
With the simple explanation:
"I do what my Father does."

Long-Ago Memories

Tonight, long-ago memories
Have been wandering down
Old familiar streets
And dark alleys
And dimly lit corridors.
With stubborn tenacity
They invade my carefully guarded defenses.
Sitting all alone watching dreams go by
I discover unexpectedly
That I am still susceptible to tears.
And then I recall vaguely
Part of an old song that says
"For these tears I died"
And my yearning heart, dear Lord
Reaches out for You.

Morbid Memories

Lord, I can't mow down morbid memories
Like my husband mows tall grass.
Mercilessly they take revenge
By tramping gleefully
Through my somber heart.
So, dear Lord
I ask YOU to shake them
In the sunlight of Your love.
Then may the gentle breeze
Of the Holy Spirit
Blow them all away—
Never to be found again.

Now

My great, strong God!
All the fight
Is drained out of me.
In my debilitating weakness
I can't even hold on to You.
But Your own words
Keep my hope stirring:
"For I your God
Am firmly grasping
Your right hand.
I am saying unto you
Do not fear.
I have become your helper."
Now, dear Lord!
Now!

Perfect Timing

O God
How perfect is Your timing!
You always seem to send
The right person at the right time.
Or a song that comforts.
Or a note that encourages.
Or somebody brings a pie
And it doesn't matter at all
That I'm not a bit hungry—
The pie spells love
And love satisfies my heart-hunger.
You fill the air with surprises
And the night with stars
And when at moments
There is the painful temptation
To give in to despair
You break through the darkness
With Your comforting words
"I'm right here."

My Personal
Rainbow

Lord, right now
I struggle with clutching fear.
Waves of agony pour over me
As I face the darkest moments
In my life's history.
But my conviction still stands firm:
You are my God!
And though I cannot predict my future
Or even tomorrow
I am sustained by the reminder
That the longest storm
The world has ever known...
And the worst...
Came to an end one clear-sky morning.
It was true for Noah
It will be true for me.
Though as yet I see no deliverance
I watch
I wait
I expect
My personal rainbow.

Surprises

Ever since I was a little girl
I've loved surprises.
Frequently my mother would say
(Her eyes twinkling)
"I've got a surprise for you!"
I'd squeal with delight
And breathlessly wait.
The surprises were never elaborate—
Often just little trinkets—
But it was the very word *surprise*
That created the ecstasy.

I'm a grown woman now
(At least chronologically)
But there is still a little girl in me
Who loves surprises.
Lord, how I thank You
For knowing me so well.
You continually surprise me with joy!

The Gift

I heard today
Of a decrepit native woman
Who walked mile after mile
Under the blistering sun
To bring a small gift of embroidery
To the missionary she deeply loved.
Hour after hour she trudged
Over rough, rugged roads
Clutching tightly her small gift.
Her weary body sagged
Her vision blurred
Her bare feet bled from the jagged rocks.

Grateful but overwhelmed
The missionary wept.
The trembling old woman spoke softly:
"Please understand.
The walk is part of the gift."

My Lord
My commitment to You is for life.
I give myself to You unreservedly
To do with me as You please.
But may I not forget
That the tears, the fears
The strain and the pain
The sunless days
The starless nights
Are all part of the whole.
In my total commitment
I give full consent:
The walk is part of the gift.